# What Others Are Saying...

Like Jim, I have advised nonprofits for more than forty years, but this book opened my eyes to rethink some of my long-held assumptions. Getting the "right" people on the board will be more successful if you redefine board development in your nonprofit to create a careful, thorough, and thoughtful process, doing your homework first. I especially loved the chapters on character, competencies, and connections. Jim illustrates his theories with real-life examples and experiences that clarify the value in a more thoughtful and thorough approach to board recruitment. He wraps it all up with a set of great self-evaluation tools that will create useful dialogue for every board. He shows us how to create a more thoughtful, progressive, and productive board recruitment program that is mission-focused and reality-based. This is a must-read that I wil recommend to all my clients!

Jean Block, nonprofit consultant, author of *The ABCs of Building Better Boards, The Invisible Yellow Line*

James Mueller is a masterful executive, board member, and high-level consultant to nonprofit organizations, and this shines through in his latest book, Onboarding Champions. He gets right into the heart of the matter in the first chapter—boom!—creating board culture, a topic that is just now starting to find its way into the boardroom.

James asks incredibly insightful questions throughout the book that can unlock strategic conversations around recruitment, selection, and onboarding of new directors—and provides practical exercises that can give insight into your own situation!

*This is also one of the very few books that look at the intersection of staff and CEO and the whole director behavior and management piece.*

*I was riveted by his stories and anecdotes, and many times nodded my head with an "I've been there too" feeling, then kept reading to see what further insights I could pick up.*

*This book will have a special place on my bookshelf and toolbox of board strategies.*

**Steven Bowman, Managing Director, Conscious Governance, Malvern, VIC, Australia**

*Finally, a book that focuses on nonprofit organizations' board composition, continuity, responsibilities, and governance from the board leadership's perspective. Mueller's book provides board leadership with the clues to recognize deficiencies in board function and performance and the tools to develop strategies and tactics to make the meaningful changes and improvements necessary to make the board an effective participant in fulfilling the organization's mission. It's a handbook that all current and future board chairs should keep close at hand.*

**Louis Bradbury, President, The Calamus Foundation**

*Whether you are with a long-established nonprofit or just beginning there is something for everyone in* **Onboarding Champions.** *Jim provides sound advice and provides best practices honed from years of professional experience. The information is timely and based on research that includes useful exercises and solutions. I highly recommend it.*

**Bradley Hurlburt, President, Community Foundation for Palm Beach and Martin Counties**

# ONBOARDING CHAMPIONS

## THE SEVEN RECRUITING PRINCIPLES OF HIGHLY EFFECTIVE NONPROFIT BOARDS

### JAMES MUELLER

THE ESSENTIAL GUIDEBOOK FOR EVERY
NONPROFIT BOARD MEMBER AND EXECUTIVE

Onboarding Champions: The Seven Recruiting Principles of Highly Effective Nonprofit Boards

by James Mueller

Published by:

James Mueller & Associates LLC

Delray Beach, Florida USA

Cover design by Margot Gassert Mueller and Stephen C. Nill
Interior design by Stephen C. Nill

ISBN: 978-1-7342973-1-7

13 12 11 10 9 8 7 6 5 4 3 2

This book takes a fresh and unique look at the challenging task of nonprofit board building. Veteran nonprofit leaders will discover many new and creative practices they can implement. Jim's focus on culture, character, competence, connections, composition, continuity, and collaboration provides a fascinating and easily understood framework of what makes an effective board of directors. Both volunteer board leaders and nonprofit professionals will find this book immensely useful in reassessing their board practices.

**Chuck Loring, CFRE, MBA, Senior Founding Partner, Loring, Sternberg & Associates, Senior Governance Associate for BoardSource**

James Mueller's book captivated me, in part because, as a consultant for almost thirty years, I think I've met clones of all the boards he has worked with. His practical advice, "what needs to be new, different, or better for the organization to thrive?" is advice well-heeded by any board. I loved his work on core values, describing them as being "in the bones." He provides practical exercises to help strengthen any board. Using his advice, you can not only assess the skills of current and potential board members but, more importantly, character! I know I will be using his book in my consulting work with boards!

**Linda Lysakowski, ACFRE, author, speaker, consultant to nonprofits**

I wish this book was published when I was an executive director. Practical and knowledgeable. Jim shows you how to navigate and affect board culture; recruit engaged, ethical, and effective board members; and create a board accepting of diversity, equity, and inclusion. James also shares how to onboard board members *to perfectly understand their roles as part of the organization's governance team. I highly recommend* **Onboarding Champions** *to both executive directors and board members.*

**Joanne Oppelt, MHA, Joanne Oppelt Consulting LLC**

*When it comes to developing high-functioning boards, the journey is the destination.* **Onboarding Champions** *charts a course for board excellence. It takes more than good intentions to successfully navigate the high seas of board recruiting and onboarding. It takes leadership, discipline, and proven techniques—all hands on deck.*

*Jim Mueller lays out in a succinct and engaging narrative—as only a person with years of deep experience and keen insight can—how to avoid common mistakes and pitfalls that undermine our best efforts. Want a great board? Recruit and onboard one because great boards don't just happen. Mediocre ones do.*

**John Popoli, President Emeritus, Lake Forest Graduate School of Management**

*Stellar recruitment is the foundation of excellent boards, and James Mueller knows how to find and retain people who will lead your organization to long-term success. His combination of case studies and practical exercises are powerful.* **Onboarding Champions** *is a resource that every board chair and nominating committee member will want by their sides.*

**Susan Schaefer, Principal, Resource Partners and co-author, *Nonprofit Board Service for the GENIUS***

# About the Author

James Mueller has been immersed in the nonprofit sector throughout his career—four decades of experience working with or serving on nonprofit boards. From higher education to health care to social service agencies, he has experienced every imaginable combination of good people doing good things through board service.

Completing his undergraduate education at Cornell University, followed by four years at a seminary, he was drawn to community service. The first ten years of his career were devoted to his undergraduate alma mater, followed by executive positions at Northwestern University, Advocate Healthcare, Lake Forest Graduate School of Management, and Goodwill Industries. After nearly thirty years in the sector, he accepted the position of COO at Grenzebach Glier & Associates, an international philanthropy consulting firm.

As the father of a son with severe physical disabilities, Mueller moved to a climate that was much kinder to his son's health complications, where he established his consulting firm, James Mueller & Associates, in 2005. In his recently released book, *Lyrics of a Broken Heart: A Father's Journey Toward Wholeness,* he writes about his very personal journey from grief to emotional wholeness.

As an author, lecturer, philanthropic and organizational strategist, and nonprofit governance expert, Mueller shares a lifetime of learning with nonprofit boards and executives. His work helping nonprofits advance their missions has earned him recognition internationally. He has worked with nonprofit board members ranging from those who have held the highest positions of success and prominence internationally—including Fortune 100 company executives, enterprise-building entrepreneurs, and legislators in Washington, DC—to local communities and neighborhoods, where good people with big hearts—whether small business owners, retailers, or company employees—ensure the health and wellbeing of their nonprofits.

James Mueller's long list of clients includes the Smithsonian, the Philadelphia 76ers, the American Association of University Professors, the Alaska Wilderness League, Florida International University, Pine Crest School, the Wilderness Land Trust, Joe DiMaggio Children's Hospital, Broward College, the Caribbean Policy Development Center, the National Museum of Health and Medicine, Selfless Love Foundation, and the Association for the Advancement of Physician and Provider Recruitment.

Mueller writes from the heart. The pages of this book are filled with intelligent and practical advice interwoven with a lifetime of stories about working with nonprofit boards.

# Dedication

To all the people who generously give their time and talent to serve on nonprofit boards. You make our communities and our world a better place. Thank you.

# Acknowledgments

John Popoli, President Emeritus, Lake Forest Graduate School of Management, for reviewing three iterations of this book, each time posing questions and offering suggestions that evoked deeper insight and clearer expression in my writing.

Eric Kelly, President of the Quantum Foundation; Jennifer Hudson, President of ThinkBeyond Public Relations; Kerry-Ann Royes, President and CEO of YWCA South Florida; and Kirk Brown, Chief Executive Officer of HANDY for taking time amid their very busy schedules to read Chapter 5 on board composition and offer counsel on diversity, inclusion, and equity. Even though I strive to embody and promote these values, their kindly delivered, thoughtful insights shed light on my own blind spots, hidden biases, and enculturated beliefs and attitudes. By helping me to grow as a person, I was able to transform the chapter. As I often tell clients, we can only see what our minds are receptive to seeing. We need moments of epiphany, when we are teleported to a new world view. At that moment, though we are standing in the same place, we see a different world. In the words of T.S. Eliot, "We shall not cease from exploration, and the end of all our exploring will be to arrive where we started and know the place for the first time." It is my hope that this chapter plays a role in catalyzing epiphanies for board members and executives.

Margot Gassert Mueller, my life partner for thirty-two years who has put up with the stresses and strains of living with a nonprofit-executive-turned-consultant spouse. Margot is extraordinarily perceptive and has not only been a great counselor but brilliant copy editor—reading chapter after chapter over and over again, shedding light on ways to organize the content, suggesting approaches to the text that more clearly communicate my intent, and flagging grammatical and typographical gremlins that haunt me.

Terrie Temkin is an expert in matters pertaining to governance who has devoted her life to serving the nonprofit sector. She is extraordinarily perceptive, well-informed, and possesses great skill in communicating ideas, concepts, and principles. Terry is also a deeply kind person who looks beyond her own challenges and needs to care for others. When I asked Terrie to review the manuscript (which I discovered was during a very challenging time), she generously agreed. Upon reading her review, I was so struck by how clearly she captured my intentions, that I asked her to write the foreword. She nailed it.

Stephen Nill, designer and editor supreme, who has provided encouragement and support throughout this process. He is a brilliant coach to whom I am deeply grateful for helping me move from an unconventional conceptual framework that existed only in my mind to a decent book that makes sense.

# Foreword

*Onboarding Champions: The Seven Recruiting Principles of Highly Effective Nonprofit Boards*, by James Mueller is a book worth your time and energy. I am confident you will feel the same if you read, digest, prioritize, and apply the ideas contained herein that you ranked as most valuable for your organization.

*Onboarding Champions* is a book of contradictions. But in this case, that's a good thing. The book is short, but it is not short on substantive content. Each page has something you can employ immediately to enhance board recruitment and ultimately the effectiveness of your board's governance. The book is clearly and simply written, but it is not a simple book. The straightforward language makes it a fast read, but the depth at which the concepts are shared will send your synapses into overdrive with their exposure to never-before-considered options. The book is steeped in research, but it is not a theoretical book. Learnings from a multitude of fields are presented as the foundation for taking a creative look at recruitment. You will recognize immediately that the ideas merit a closer look because they did not just come out of the author's head, but rather are based on evidence—evidence validated by work done from various perspectives and tested over the years. Finally, the ideas presented are familiar, but the recommended applications in many cases are new. You will sense that by merely tweaking some of your go-to approaches the results are likely to be very different.

As purely a governance consultant since 1994, I have found a lot of information "out there" about recruiting and onboarding board directors. In fact, when initially asked to review this book I inwardly groaned. I'll admit that my first thought was, "Oh boy, not another book on recruitment." Yet, I recognize that people are intensely interested in this topic. In working with clients—regardless of why I have been hired to partner with them—it is the topic that everyone most wants to talk about. Clearly, in a lot of cases what's "out there" is not working and those serving on boards are looking for more helpful answers. I can honestly say, Jim's approach is refreshingly practical and realistic.

He doesn't offer a magic wand…he unequivocally states that cultural and organizational transformation requires work and that it could take three years for the nature of a board to change. But he also makes you believe that such transformation is possible. He presents the best definition of core values I've seen and if readers simply buy into that, they will see a positive change in their organizations. He took the initiative to ask Black colleagues how he could present issues of diversity, inclusion and racial equity that were more meaningful and potentially effective than those typically presented by well-meaning but culturally clueless White sector leaders. So, if like me, you are one of those well-intentioned leaders who makes diversity a priority and always tries to use the right language but still finds themselves recruiting Black board directors that don't stay, this book may provide valuable insights to help turn that situation around.

If you are one of those that learns best from case studies, you will find this book particularly instructive. Jim includes numerous examples of the good, the bad, and the ugly from his own vast experience as a board director, a board chair, a senior development director, a CEO, and a consultant. He provides helpful exercises that may sound like something your consultant facilitated at the last retreat, to little avail. But these exercises will actually move the needle if they are debriefed as he suggests.

What I believe Jim accomplishes most successfully with the book is piloting the readers through a process he recommends to leaders looking to create change: He 'pays attention to the elasticity of their imagination.'

Terrie Temkin, Ph.D.
Founding Principal
CoreStrategies for Nonprofits, Inc.

# Contents

# Preface

I've been working with governing boards for over four decades. Hard to believe. It seems like such a short time ago that I was sitting in the office of a nonprofit as a summer intern. One afternoon I was asked to speak with members of the board about an issue that had arisen regarding the long-time CEO, a sweet man who had served the organization for a few decades. He wasn't adapting well to the changes in the organization. Several months later, under pressure from the board, he resigned, devastated. Looking back over the years, I have wondered if there was something I could have done differently to help him.

Four years later, after graduate school, I found myself back in the nonprofit sector, working as a county staff associate for the federal government's cooperative extension program. I had some interactions with the board as a staff associate, but for the most part, I only knew them as kind people, wonderful volunteers with the best of intentions. I also learned that each saw the world differently, each brought their own values and beliefs about what was right. And I watched my CEO, another kind, salt-of-the-earth man, try to negotiate those personalities. He wasn't adept at social politics and lost his job within the next year.

Being young in my career, these two experiences were quite provocative. It wasn't just that two competent CEO's lost their jobs because they lost the confidence of their boards. It was the realization that volunteers—most with little to no training—hold the most powerful position in the nonprofit world. *The fate of nonprofits is in their hands.* This epiphany transformed how I viewed my future in the nonprofit sector.

The first thing that occurred to me was that I needed to get to know the members of the board. Even though I was a few professional levels away from interacting with the board, I decided to get to know them as people, to connect, to understand them… and respect their points of view, even when I didn't agree. I became interested in figuring out what boards are supposed to do, what makes them effective, and how to work collaboratively with them.

This served me well later on as a senior executive in higher education and health care because I had learned a lot about identifying the right volunteer leaders. I learned not to recruit the first willing soul because that could come back to haunt me. I learned that business acumen was important, but it didn't translate directly into governing competence. I learned that being a leader in the community didn't always translate into board effectiveness. I learned that popularity didn't always translate into character. And I learned that just because someone was well connected didn't always mean they would use those connections for the cause of my organization.

When I began serving on boards, I gained even further insight into how boards function—or how they magnify dysfunction. Across all of the organizations where I served as a board member, few of my fellow board members really understood the job. Though often good-hearted, there were huge gaps in their governing competence.

This is not true of all boards. In my consulting practice, I have seen very high-functioning boards. And I have come to understand what makes them great.

Exceptional boards are not the result of lucky happenstance. They are carefully crafted and cared for.

# Introduction

Nonprofit boards are champions of the public's trust. They are established to ensure that the cause for which the nonprofit was awarded its tax-exempt status is pursued with integrity and excellence. That the nonprofit stays true to its mission and fulfills its purpose. That those intended to be served through its work receive programs and services that address their needs.

Nonprofit boards are also champions of the mission and vision of the nonprofits they serve. Nonprofits exist in a space where normal market forces cannot sustain a for-profit entity. For example, there is no money to be made in feeding the hungry who cannot afford a meal, or housing single mothers who earn minimum wage, or providing support services for low income elderly with limited mobility, or taking care of the medical needs of those who are indigent.

The complexities and challenges of sustaining a nonprofit far exceed those faced by similar-sized for-profit entities. Board members are called upon to be voices in their communities, to promote the importance of their cause, and to attract a band of true believers so that their nonprofits have the best opportunity to have the greatest impact for the most people.

The responsibility of board members for proper oversight is quite similar between the for-profit and nonprofit sectors, and business leaders who volunteer to serve bring significant strengths to nonprofit governance. Nevertheless, there is a significant difference in the motives and purposes. While both are responsible for ensuring sound management practices, for-profit governance is concerned with the interests of shareholders, nonprofit governance is concerned with delivering mission-centered results both for those it serves and for the greater public good.

Let me offer two examples of nonprofit mission-driven management.

Let's say you are on the board of a food pantry. The pantry receives an offer from a food supplier to provide a truckload of products for just the cost of delivery. On close examination, you discover that the nutritional value is substandard, and the food is laced with additives that you know are not healthy. No one knows this but you. If you accept the delivery, it makes the organization look savvy and successful and strengthens your relationship with the supplier, who might provide sponsorships down the road. Yet, if you are true to the mission, "to provide healthy, nutritious meals," you reject the offer even though it is the more challenging path to take. And you do so because you are champions of the public trust.

Here is another. A nearly one-hundred-year-old organization wants to take a fresh look at its values, vision, and mission. After a series of in-depth sessions with the staff and board, a set of core values, a new mission statement, a brand position statement, and a vision statement are defined. The vision statement creates healthy debate and engaging conversations throughout the organization. In its simplicity, it is powerful: "No one is homeless."

But what does this have to do with being a champion of the public trust? That simple statement was taken very seriously by the CEO and his board. One day he told me that it caused him to rework some of his core programs. He realized the organization was not being true to its vision if they turned people away because their behavior was either violent or unmanageable. He pondered, "How can I say we are committed to no one being homeless if we turn away those who are most difficult to serve." As a result, the organization started exploring alternatives with law enforcement and other agencies to develop options to serve those whom they formerly turned away.

The organization didn't need to add this additional challenge to its workload. But the CEO and the board weren't focused on what was expedient for the organization. Instead, they were champions of those they serve and the public trust. .

How do we create and sustain a board of champions?

Recruitment and onboarding are the most fundamental and critical factors in creating a competent, effective board that serves the needs of the organization's constituents. As Jim Collins advocates in *Good to Great: Why Some Companies Make the Leap and Others Don't*, it has a lot to do with getting the right people in the right seats on the right bus. So many of our nonprofit boards pay little attention to this critical aspect of creating a high-performing governing board. Even though serving as a board member is the highest office and most powerful position in the nonprofit sector.

Every board member brings whom they are to the boardroom. For better or for worse, boards experience only what a person is capable of offering. So, choose well. And to do so, you must know what talent you need, know how to identify that talent in the people you seek, and know how to bring them aboard effectively.

Most boards are populated by smart, committed people who are hungry to learn and grow. Through my engagements with boards, I continue to learn and grow along with them. As I tell my clients, there are many paths up the mountain to arrive at the destination of a highly effective nonprofit board. What I write about in this book is the pathway I have found—sometimes created—to get to the top of the mountain.

The seven principles form a guidebook, a traveler's log, a reflection upon what I have learned over several decades. They are not directives, but offerings for you to consider. As you reflect on them, they may evoke even better ideas than I have presented. If that is the case, I have succeeded. And please share them with me. There is always room for improvement.

## My Approach to Writing This Book

I find that stories connect us to the lived experience in a way that a simple narrative cannot. They give us a feel for real people grappling with real issues, and I hope this approach helps you feel more connected to the material. I've used italicized font to set the stories apart from the commentary and connect them as they are woven throughout the text.

I have drawn upon a lifetime of personal experiences in writing this book. In the stories I tell, I have edited details and changed names and locales to assure confidentiality. In a few instances, I have created a composite from different experiences to clarify the point I am trying to make.

Chapter five addresses issues of diversity, inclusion, and equity. Implicit in the discussion is respect for racial and ethnic identity. As I discussed drafts of this chapter with friends and colleagues, I came to understand the importance of capitalization regarding racial identity—and how it is a complex issue. As my editor commented, the English language is a moving target. Even the experts on grammar and word usage do not agree, and recognized experts have changed their opinions in the last few months. After significant research on the topic and polling of Black and White colleagues, I decided to capitalize words that identify race as that is the majority opinion in both research and polling.

A note about gender. Over the last decade, gender identity has become more fluid—or at least we are now beginning to recognize people whose gender identity is non-binary. As I explored this issue, I discovered, with the help of my daughter, that it is polite to ask whether someone prefers to be "he," "she," or "they." I have been told that it is one of the simplest and most important ways to show respect for someone's identity. Further, most major grammar sources, including the Chicago Manual of Style and the Associated Press, have determined "they" is acceptable for referring to a non-binary person.

As I wrote the stories that illustrate the concepts of each chapter, I grappled with the issue of whether to use "they" when referring to a singular person. When I attempted to simply insert "they" for "she" or "he" I encountered more complications and readers who skipped over these two explanatory paragraphs would likely assume I made grammatical errors. For example, changing "she" to "they" in one section results in, "they is highly competent." After much thought I concluded, since throughout the book I refer to a singular person by binary gender, I would use the traditional binary pronoun.

The overall format for the book is constructed in a manner that makes it easy for you to remember the concepts and understand how to apply them. One approach I employ is to provide definitions for the words that define each of the chapters. My intention in using definitions is to establish a mutual frame of reference and to provide clarity and focus regarding the content of each chapter. Because each chapter is built on the meaning of the chapter's title word, I thought it important to establish my definition of its meaning at the outset. I hope you find this helpful.

You needn't read the entire book to begin to make changes in your boards' practices. Each chapter addresses an essential component of recruitment and onboarding. So, jump to a section that addresses a challenge that you may be facing. I have also included a self-assessment tool in the last chapter that you can use with your board. It is intended to stimulate reflection and discussion.

This book is intentionally not long. My aim is to keep it accessible through the stories I tell and practical by including exercises throughout. My hope is that this approach makes the book an easy-reference guide. As such, you might find it useful as a reference to include with your board member materials—or as part of your board member orientation reading. It can be used as a reference that facilitates open, candid communication when discussing board member expectations.

Though you can jump from topic to topic as needed, there is a benefit to starting with the first chapter and working through the chapters sequentially, as each chapter builds upon the information that comes before.

The chapters are laid out in logical order, from understanding and managing board culture to creating a board member recruitment profile, to managing composition (diversity and inclusion), to achieving continuity (alignment between board members competencies, knowledge, and understanding of their role and the organization's needs). The final section of the book addresses the importance of collaboration—among board members, between the board and the staff, and among organizations.

By giving serious consideration to each of these principles, you can create a healthy, high-functioning, effective governing board.

## Part One

# RECRUITMENT

# CHAPTER 1

# Culture

Culture: the unspoken assumptions about how people should think, feel, and act—and the behaviors that result from those assumptions.

*She is smart, strategic, and analytical. As an executive who had ascended to the top of her profession in the rarified air of one of the top multinational technology companies founded in America, she is highly competent and community-minded— an extraordinary catch for any organization's board. And my client was the lucky beneficiary.*

*She demonstrated her value to the organization almost imme-diately—diving in, she accepted committee responsibilities, organized budget projections, and provided a framework for strategy development. I attended the board meeting where she made the presentation of her recommendations.*

*The next day, she resigned.*

*A few weeks before this meeting, the board chair had reached out to me to discuss his concerns about board composition and effectiveness. He recognized problems, particularly with communication, but also with the general cohesiveness of the board. His underlying concern was the board's culture, or as I defined at the opening, the unspoken assumptions about how people should think, feel, and act and the behaviors that result from those assumptions.*

Every board has a culture—either by default or intention. I work with boards to achieve intentional culture. Even though culture has such a direct effect on board performance, few boards address it. Is it because they aren't aware that boards have their own unique cultures? Or that they are not aware of its impact? Or do they feel ill-equipped to deal with it? Whatever the reason, unless someone calls attention to the underlying habits, assumptions, and practices, an organization will continue to be stymied by a dysfunctional culture.

Healthy cultures are inquisitive and invite diverse perspectives and debate. They embrace generative and strategic thinking. Innovation is valued. In healthy cultures, board members work collaboratively and with humility to solve problems. Members understand their governance oversight responsibilities. They respect the role of management and form a constructive partnership with the CEO. They are intellectually and emotionally invested in the cause they serve and are its champions.

A fundamental responsibility of a board chair is to attend to culture, to keep it healthy and productive. As my dear friend John

Popoli, president emeritus of Lake Forest Graduate School of Management, puts it: "Modeling good culture through behavior is everyone's job, starting with the chair." Competent organizational governance starts with self-governance.

One of my tasks, when invited to provide governance counsel, is to help the leadership team recognize the existence of culture and the impact it is having on the organization.

Reorienting or reinventing a productive, conscious culture cannot happen overnight. It requires board members to recognize the problematic culture, and once they recognize its consequences, accept that it must change, and commit to implementing change.

*Recognition* usually occurs in one of two ways: either the more astute board members become aware that something is amiss (as with our board chair in the example above) and take action or, usually, more often, the organization is in crisis or encounters a situation that threatens its viability.

*Acceptance* is the agreement among stakeholders that behaviors and practices must change.

*Commitment* ensures that the process of change moves forward. It requires stakeholders to commit to a new course of action, create processes to make that happen, and assign accountabilities. This creates the pathway to a healthy, intentional culture.

So, what happened to our tech exec? She didn't fit with the culture. Her style was dramatically different from anyone else on the board, and I suspect she recognized this pretty quickly. Her skills were undervalued, and her contributions not appreciated. She came from a very different world than her board colleagues. While her everyday work world was technology and strategy with a focus on data-driven decisions, her colleagues were entrepreneurs and cause advocates. Her highly structured approach to decision-making collided with their creative and intuitive approach.

Not embracing her style and contributions was not intentional by her fellow board members; they just didn't recognize what she was contributing. I suspect that no one but the chair and I understood why she left. And this was confirmed by the assessment tool we employed with the board, the results of which I reported at the same meeting.

It was a great loss that could have been avoided if members had been attuned to their decision-making styles and understood how to appreciate the great value that she brought.

While this outcome was disappointing, it could have been avoided. Board members who understand culture and are aware of its functioning within their nonprofits have a range of options. In recent years, I have been on a journey with two organizations that have completely transformed their cultures and reinvented themselves. Through this process we were changing the old guard's assumptions about the association's culture—how people should think, feel, and act as governance leaders. For each, the result is a new, powerful trajectory that has yielded significant growth in value to those they serve. This happened because they understood and managed their culture.

*One of these organizations, a national professional membership organization, was floundering, struggling to remain relevant in a dynamic environment that threatened to leave it behind. This was an association of professionals that started to experience fracturing among its membership and competition from other corporate organizations that offered programs that threatened the value of its offerings to its members. Throughout the process I describe below, the change agents and champions were in constant tension with an old guard that liked things as they had always been. The challenge to the change agents was to not lose the connection to the old guard while they reached for a new identity. (I understand culture and identity are separate concepts. In this instance, culture was impeding movement toward a new identity.) The phrase I often use when talking to the champions of change is "pay attention to the elasticity of their imagination." That is, don't go too quickly or too far to a new horizon, keep engaging the old guard in conversation about the shared vision that will draw them forward to a vibrant and relevant association that is positioned at the forefront of its field.*

*Within this organization, the old guard was nostalgic for the good old days, and they would often recount how the organization was founded. Because we were aware of this, in our discussions, we didn't cut short their reminiscences, but rather pulled from their language ideas for the new vision. I would take time to draw out what they had envisioned at the founding and why. I would then apply those concepts to the current situation. For instance, when they described those they served "in the good old days," I would ask, "why?" And as they described their why, I would ask how the environment is different today, and to achieve their "why" in today's environment, are there others that they serve—and other ways to serve them? This approach worked very well because we led them through a logical process of effective inquiry—never stretching their imaginations too far.*

*Among the board members was an individual who accepted the responsibility for board development and strategic planning. As with the board chair mentioned in the opening of this chapter, this individual recognized that something was amiss. He quietly questioned leadership assumptions and governance practices that he believed fell short of governance responsibilities and were a failure of board leadership.*

*For convenience's sake, let's call him "Pat." Pat recognized the need for an external ally and governance expert to help bring about a new level of consciousness among his fellow board members. He needed to convince other members that something in the culture was sabotaging the organization's ability to thrive.*

As an agent of change—either as an insider, like Pat, or as an external consultant—it is important to first assess the board's self-understanding, its awareness of the need for change, its receptivity for change, and its capacity to change.

In assessing the board's awareness of dysfunctional culture and the need for change, always start by seeking answers to the questions that will bring clarity. Are they aware of any threats to the organization's viability? Are their perceptions of the organization's viability aligned with the realities beyond the boardroom? Are they attuned to the business, economic, and cultural shifts that, if unaddressed, will cause the organization to become irrelevant? Are they mindful of the opinions of external business thought leaders who influence perceptions of the organization? Are they even aware of one another's points of view on these issues?

Assessing receptivity: Do board members listen to other points of view? Are they willing to question their own positions on issues?

Do they seek outside counsel? Have they admitted that they might not see the whole picture? Are they able to recognize their personal biases and respond objectively?

Assessing competence: Do board members have a firm grasp of the responsibilities of governance? Do they possess the expertise to effectively address the challenges at hand? Do they have sufficient information? Are they able to engage one another in effective deliberation? Do they understand their oversight responsibilities?

I have found that the best way to reveal answers to these questions is through carefully structured group conversations as well as confidential individual interviews with each of the members. I start with an approach I call "positive inquiry coaching." Positive inquiry starts with respect for the individual, and an assumption that all board members are doing their very best. So, I formulate questions to reveal beliefs, attitudes, and knowledge.

I begin by asking about their aspirations, starting with general, then moving to more specific, questions. For instance, I often begin with: Why do you serve on the board? What do you hope to contribute? What do you hope to achieve? How do you envision your responsibilities? What are the attributes of a great board? What do you hold each other accountable to achieve? What would you like the board to do that is new, different, or better than it is doing now?

*In the pre-retreat board member interviews for this association, I started out by asking a handful of critical questions: What is working well right now? What are the most important and/or challenging issues facing the association? What are the key governance issues and/or challenges facing the board? What governance issues do you believe we should address in our first session at the retreat? If there was anything you would change to make this board excel, what would it be? At the end of the retreat, what would you like to take away? Is there anything you think I should know (as the consultant) in preparing for the retreat?*

*I designed each question to reveal board members' beliefs about their roles and responsibilities—how they think, feel, and act. Were the association issues they perceived as challenging falling within the purview of governance—or seen from a governance perspective? Were the governance issues actual governance issues? In terms of takeaways, are they seeking greater governance competence? As far as "anything else you think I should know," it is always good to ask a question that will evoke a response about other issues that are bothering board members.*

*In a debrief with Pat, I shared that only two board members were concerned that governance was falling short of its responsibilities. The rest of the members, to a person, viewed the solution to the organization's challenges as finding more reliable volunteers.*

The manner in which most board members thought, felt, and acted in regard to their responsibilities was ineffectual. They had not established an effective board culture. Most were not inquisitive, or innovative, or concerned about proper governance. They were in the dark. But they were not alone.

*A few years ago, I was called by a board chair of another nonprofit. She was a successful advertising executive who was very frustrated by the inexperience of her board colleagues. Together we devised a two-day strategic planning retreat, using a well-tested format designed to elicit fresh perspectives and new ideas. We also wove in governance education sessions.*

*At the end of the first afternoon, the board chair came up to me and said, "I can see it in your eyes, this isn't working." With a deep sigh and a shrug, I said, "Time to reinvent the agenda." Then we both laughed at our predicament, an unspoken acknowledgment that a culture of lax thinking was smothering our retreat.*

*I asked her, "Who do you know in this world that is doing innovative things? Who is shaking things up? Who has a passion for the kind of work this organization does?"*

*That night we reached out to a few nonprofit executives and board members who fit the bill. Two accepted our invitation to attend the retreat the next day as guests. In our briefing, we described our challenge and asked them to just be themselves and speak with candor.*

*At the retreat, we introduced them and described their accomplishments in the community. We placed them on panels with other board members, and we also set up a discussion where board members were encouraged to ask them anything that had to do with the role of governance in their organizations.*

*Though we knew this was out of the ordinary for this group, it worked because we carefully staged the session and guided the discussion. We knew what we needed to elicit in terms of best and proven practices. And these highly competent executives and volunteers were selected because they under-stood the principles of effective governance.*

*The fresh perspectives of these two outsiders jolted the group out of its lethargy, opened up the discussion, and new ideas flooded in. One crucial element that contributed to the success was the sense of humor and openness that they brought to the discussion. Because the guests didn't have an agenda, and they weren't trying to teach anyone anything, the members of the board were receptive and responsive.*

Back to my work with the association. In that case, I did not have access to outside organizational peers, so I devised a twofold agenda for the first retreat. I made a case for sound governance practices and facilitated a discussion to explore and articulate board members' understanding of the organization's core values.

Throughout the retreat, I was able to assess individual board members' awareness, receptivity, and competence. By doing so, I was able to probe areas, ask clarifying questions, and coach them, all while educating them on effective governance, organizational identity, and problem-solving.

To give you a sense of what I mean, I started by asking, "what needs to be new, different, or better for the organization to thrive?" Answers to this question helped me understand whether members were thinking tactically or strategically. For those who said, "recruit and retain more members," I would ask clarifying questions like, "What do you think members are seeking from the association?" "What do your most-preferred members look like?" "In what ways can the association adapt or change its offerings to attract most-preferred members?" "Are there perception-related issues that might keep preferred members from joining?"

Through these discussions we were able to loosen up beliefs of the old guard and reached an agreement that the association needed to do several things differently or better to achieve substantive systemic change. Some important agreements from the early meetings included: reposition the brand, deliver our member assets more effectively, demonstrate our value, and develop new leadership aligned with the demands of our current marketplace.

This was the beginning of a three-year cultural and organizational transformation process that I will revisit later in the book. And in that third year I was able to introduce an external professional peer to this group. The purpose was to help them see their blind spots regarding their association's value and contribution to the field.

I found it interesting and somewhat troubling that some board members didn't immediately understand the value of this outside professional's perspective and were resistant. It took a while for me to convince them that this person would present a view that might help them break free of limiting assumptions (an expression of their existing culture) that I knew were holding them back. When I was finally able to get them to consent and receive the feedback, it was an epiphany. It seeded in their thinking a pathway to transform the way they saw themselves and set them on course to reimagine not only governance but the very nature of the organization. Once all of the board members heard the outside professional's perspective, they recognized that the association had much more value to many more people than they had realized.

## Shaping Culture Through Core Values

While sound governance practices create the environment for effective organizational leadership, when it comes to managing culture, core values are fundamental. Research demonstrates that if we understand our core values, make them explicit, and attend to them, we can create and sustain a productive culture in the boardroom—and throughout the organization.

So, what are core values? Core values determine how an organization acts in the world, from the formation of its vision and mission to the way it constructs and delivers its programs and services. They are *not* something toward which an organization aspires; rather, they are what it embodies, what it lives. They must be authentic and be reflected in the organization's practices and behaviors—from the members of the board, to the staff, to the volunteers.

Sometimes we confuse core values with principles of behavior, like the oft-repeated Boy Scouts oath, which states that a Boy Scout is trustworthy, loyal, helpful, friendly, courteous, kind, obedient, cheerful, thrifty, brave, clean, and reverent. Boy Scouts commit to acting out these behaviors in deeds and actions. What the principles don't describe is what makes a great Boy Scout tick. In his research into valuing and the hierarchy of values at Vanderbilt and the University of Tennessee, Dr. Robert Hartman showed that our core values precede our behaviors and determine how we think, feel, and act. So, while one may commit to a set of principles, that motivation is temporal, it's not in the bones. Core values are in the bones.

Core values go deep. For an organization, they are the beliefs in which it is rooted; beliefs about what is good and right, the essence of its brand, and the norms that guide its business practices. They are the values that compel the organization and its stakeholders to do great work. They are distinctive to the organization and differentiate it from its peers.

You might even say that core values call nonprofits into existence—because the founders felt an obligation to create an organization that would address the gap between "what is" and "what should be." When members of an organization's leadership team understand its distinctive core values, they gain greater clarity about how to make decisions and how to consistently convert their resources into effective action.

At the moment a board decides to revisit its core values—or articulate them for the first time, it is essential to achieve clarity and alignment among board members so that when it comes time to focus, everyone is in agreement. Board members must first agree on how to describe "what should be" for those the organization serves. As people answer this question, they are speaking from their beliefs and values about what is good and right—even though they haven't yet articulated those underlying values. The second discussion question is: "What is causing the gap between 'what is' and 'what should be?'" "What evidence do we all agree supports our case?" "What facts can we articulate?" This process helps the discussion steer clear of personal bias.

This conversation is a precursor to the following exercise.

## Practical Exercise

Take a moment to think about your own values. Start by just writing them down stream-of-consciousness one after another. Let it flow, don't censor. What I think you will find is that it may take longer to write down the next value as you go further into the process. But the values will begin to have a more specific meaning or definition because you are asking, "What shapes me and the way I think?" As you continue writing, ask yourself *why*—"why is that my value?" As you do so, other values will come to mind. In pursuing a line of questioning, I suggest you ask yourself "why" up to seven times, as it will deepen your thinking.

For example, you might start with values like love, kindness, honesty, caring, integrity. These are quite common. But when you get to the end of this easy list, as you think a little longer, you will come up with some that are uniquely yours. Let's try the "why" exercise. Why love, for example. Because it is fundamental to a life well-lived. Why? Because it is the cornerstone of happiness. Why? Because it is important that I am a good person. Why? Because goodness is at the core of my being.

Let's look at where we are. We started with the easy value of love, which is a general, common concept shared by most people. But as we probed, we discovered other values of "a life well-lived," "happiness," "good person," and "goodness." These are unique, personal values. And we asked why only four times. Further, upon reflection, you might decide that it feels as if there is something more. Take a break and, when you come back and are in a refreshed state of mind, ask "why." You will likely discover something even deeper.

In addition to the "why" exercise, there are other ways to probe your core values. Allow yourself some time. Think about those you love… what guides your feelings, thoughts, and actions toward them. Those are your values. Think about those who may have hurt your feelings… what values guide your feelings, thoughts, actions, and reactions. Think about where you volunteer… where you socialize… and, to some extent, where you work. The way you think, feel, and act in each of these situations is determined by your core values.

Once you have your list, take a few moments to reflect on it. Does it seem authentic? Complete? How do the various values you've listed make you feel?

Everyone can discover their unique core values if they take a little time and probe a bit below the surface.

Now for the next step. Circle the ones that resonate most strongly. From that list, pick the top three and define what they mean to you, even in just a sentence. This last exercise will help you clarify what is important to you about that value.

During the next week, carry the list of values that you identified that are most resonant. As you go throughout your days—good times, tough times, what do you notice? Are your values consistent with your thoughts and behavior? Did you think about adjusting your behaviors? Did you think about adjusting your values?

Most of us experience some dissonance between what we say we believe and how we act. This is a wonderful exercise for greater self-awareness. The research on values and behaviors indicates that we can achieve alignment through making our core values explicit—writing them down—and consciously taking actions each day that are consistent with them.

## Organizational Values

In the perfect world, every board should take time to identify its organization's core values. I suggest conducting the personal exercise first because it gives you a feel for the potential if you apply the same discipline to the board exercise.

A good starting place for an organizational exercise is to understand what core values are not. Often board members will say that their organization's core values include honesty, flexibility, raising money, serving more people, being receptive to change, community service, and so on. These are important practices and principles, so why aren't they usually core values?

First, you must be selective when choosing your final list of core values. If you choose too many or choose values shared by several other organizations, you dilute your identity and lose an opportunity to convey your brand. Your core values set you apart. They are an opportunity to make a memorable statement.

You are probably asking, why isn't community service a core value? Or honesty? Let me ask you: among all the charitable organizations in the sector, which shouldn't be invested in community service? Which shouldn't be honest? Or transparent? Which shouldn't be focused on raising money or serving people? Which shouldn't be receptive to change? Though these are important, they are characteristics common to most nonprofit organizations.

Identifying core values takes a soul-searching, open-minded debate among the organization's leadership team. You need to dig in and ask, "What is at the core of our identity? What differentiates us and defines our essence and purpose? What values will immediately communicate who we are to anyone who reads them?"

*Several years ago, I worked with an organization whose mission was to help the elderly and those in financial distress to maintain and repair their homes. Working with a board of only a handful of individuals, this small band of volunteers came up with the most memorable core values I have encountered in all of my work over decades: dignity and restoration. These two words define their essence and purpose. Who would have thought to fix a toilet or repair a roof had anything to do with dignity and restoration… until you take a closer look.*

26

*These devoted volunteers understood that people take pride in
their homes, that when they cannot afford to repair them, it
affects their sense of well-being. And so, they understood that
they weren't just repairing homes; they were restoring lives.
And those truly are core values.*

Let's get back to the story about the professional membership
association. What happened at that retreat?

Using a construction metaphor, you have to excavate before
you can lay a solid foundation. So, we questioned assumptions,
confronted old thought patterns, and dug deep into beliefs and
values—the underpinnings of the organization. At the end of the
retreat, we had four core values.

Once we had those values defined, we had a shared understanding of what the organization stands for. With that footing, we
were able to debate whether the organization was living its values
through its actions, from program offerings to staff performance
to board member recruitment and behavior.

By carefully articulating and defining its core values—the roots
of its culture—the organization could imagine a different future. It
transformed itself from an inward-facing, insular organization that
was becoming irrelevant to an outward-facing organization with
a crystal-clear identity—which resulted in a new vision, mission,
value proposition, priorities, and infrastructure. With this new
self-awareness, the association understood that a new leadership
culture needed to be established, redefining the character and
competencies that board members need to possess to lead the
organization through the difficult process of restructuring and
recapturing relevance within its profession.

When recruiting new members, boards should have the organization's core values foremost in mind, using them as a guide to identify candidates that embrace the organization's core values and intentional culture. In this environment, every new recruit is oriented to the organization's values, what they mean, their obligation to embody them, and how they are made explicit in the boardroom and throughout the organization.

When determining core values, a great place to start, as noted above, is setting the parameters of what they are not. Values are not core values if they are generic or too general, if they are commonly used in the sector to describe several organizations, if they are not distinctive to the organization, if they do not differentiate the organization from its peers, or if they do not define the core identity of the organization.

## Practical Exercise

How do I identify my organization's core values?

There are several ways to approach this process, but most importantly, don't rush it. Once you have an initial set of values, take time to step back and reflect. Make sure the list authentically captures your true core values. I recommend using trained consultants for this process because they bring an objective point of view and are free of the political and hierarchal concerns that may limit an insider's effectiveness.

The exercise I outline here works well with boards because it is succinct and produces statements that are easy to grasp and understand.

It is important to engage both members of the board and members of the staff in this process. Depending upon the board-staff dynamics, you can conduct this exercise either as one group or as separate groups. If the latter, the two sets of values need to be integrated through a process of comparing, discussing, refining, and formally adopting. No matter how you compose the group(s), the process is the same.

Divide the large group into small discussion groups of four to six people.

Assign a facilitator and recorder to each group. The facilitator is responsible for keeping the discussion on track, drawing out those who may be silent, managing those who dominate the conversation and clarifying statements to ensure correct understanding and agreement.

The recorder must ensure that the offerings of each participant are captured through clear, concise notetaking. This individual is also responsible for making sure the final decisions of the group are recorded legibly on a flip chart for presentation. Or has typed them to share on screen for a video conference.

Once in the small groups, participants contribute to making a list of what they believe are the organization's core values. (I recommend taking a few minutes at the outset for group members to write down their lists of values privately—and then share with the group. This supports independent thinking, which improves the process.)

The process works best if participants focus on one word for each value, rather than a phrase. Usually, nouns work the best. The nuance of any word can be drawn out and made explicit when the values are defined at the end of the process.

After a few minutes, the facilitator of the small group leads a discussion of each participant's core values that have been shared with the group.

The facilitator looks to the participants to describe what their values mean to them and why they offered them. Go around the group, asking each participant to describe one value. Repeat this cycle until all have placed values on the list.

The facilitator then invites all small group participants to comment on what they like on the list and encourages them to ask clarifying questions.

As the discussion progresses, groups can integrate similar values—with the permission of those who placed those values on the list.

The facilitator then helps the group identify a handful of top values. During this process, the group may again discover it can combine values into one word that captures the meaning of several values. Whatever the case, only the person who places a value on the list has the authority to remove it or combine it with another.

When the small groups finish their discussions, reconvene the large group where each small group presents its set of core values. Then facilitate a discussion to compare small group findings and use a process similar to the small group discussion to reduce the list to the three to five top core values that resonate with the entire group.

Once the values are sorted and prioritized through whole group discussion, assign a task group to define each value and its meaning to the organization. A formula that works well is using two sentences. The first sentence describes the definition of the word. The second describes how the organization applies this value.

Here are examples from the foundation I chaired that supports arts education for elementary school students:

*Inspiration* (is the value)*: To breathe in, to envision, to imagine possibilities beyond one's circumstances, to aspire toward one's highest potential* (is the definition). *The Foundation invests in opportunities for children—their families and our community—to dream about and create hope-filled, productive, satisfying futures through arts education* (is the application).

*Self-Expression: To express one's own personality, feelings, or ideas. The foundation invests in opportunities for children to become creatively engaged in education and the arts; to have outlets to express their ideas, feelings, interests, and imagination.*

*Character: To develop beliefs, values, and ethics that support a meaningful, joyful life. The foundation invests in opportunities for children that foster qualities of respect, humility, confidence, self-esteem, and leadership.*

Every nonprofit should post its values on the boardroom walls, or as a background to video conference calls, so they are in full view at every board meeting. Post them in the public areas of the organization, in the staff lunchroom, on the website, and in publications. Through a clear understanding of its values and constant conscious alignment with them, an organization can create collegial enthusiasm and deepen morale. By understanding and attending to an organization's core values, boards foster the right culture, not only in the boardroom but throughout the organization.

# CHAPTER 2

# Character

Character: who we are behind our social masks and what shows up when the pressure is on.

*"She what?!?!?!" Those were the first words out of my mouth as I grappled with regaining my composure. How? Why? No way. Really? Oh, my god. I know this person… I thought.*

*When I served in a district office for a prominent institution several years ago, one of my responsibilities was to provide guidance and support to alumni clubs throughout the region. It was important to cultivate a strong presence for the institution and, with alumni, demonstrate the character of our graduates so we could build a strong, unblemished brand and respectable presence—as a backdrop to our student recruitment and fundraising. The alumni formed clubs in each major city that were organized with their own boards of directors. These clubs helped interview prospective students and handled the phones for the annual appeal.*

*One day I received a call from the president of one club. The treasurer had emptied the club's treasury and disappeared. I had known this individual—I thought I knew her well—and I was so surprised to hear the news. But, when I thought about it, I really didn't know her. She was friendly and had helped me out when I visited the city on institutional business.*

*Upon reflection, I realized that I had made assumptions about her character based on several polite, casual interactions. So did the club's leadership. In retrospect, no one really knew a lot about her. She was an alum. That was her credential. Alums are supposed to be people of high moral character. We all learned that wasn't true—and from that moment forward, I more deeply understood how important it is to replace assumptions with due diligence.*

We see people's character reflected in their actions in the world—and we usually judge them... as good or bad, caring or uncaring, thoughtful or thoughtless. How board members conduct themselves will ultimately reflect upon the organization—from the public perception of the organization to the reputation of the board itself... and its ability to recruit new members and raise financial support.

It is important to screen for character during the board member recruitment process. Yet, how many boards do? Most often, it's ignored, and too often, assumptions are made of a person's character based upon the first impression or just because of their willingness to serve on the board. Asking board members to assess character in the recruitment process may feel like too much of a hassle, or board members don't want to feel embarrassed by checking up on someone they may know socially or through their businesses. Nevertheless, it remains a critical factor. And I suggest that when done well, investigating character has the opposite effect. It communicates that the organization is serious about selecting the right individuals to serve on its board. In my experience, it doesn't upset prospective members; instead, it communicates that serving on this board is serious business.

*Several years ago, I was asked to serve on a board. I liked the organization, and I had a great deal of respect for the person who approached me. She knew of my expertise in governance and thought I could be helpful in the board's development.*

*Within a few days, I received a thick packet of materials about the organization—history, strategic plan, programs, staffing, board responsibilities, etc. In that packet was a several-page application for board membership that required three references—and a background check.*

*After I submitted the application, they contacted me with a request to have breakfast with the CEO, the chair of the board, and the chair of the development committee. During the conversation, they asked me to tell them about my perception of the organization and what I thought I could contribute.*

*Within a week after that conversation, I received calls from two of my references saying, "Hey, this organization takes this seriously." Within the next week, I had an extensive conversation with the CEO regarding what she needed and expected from the board and what she thought I could contribute.*

*By the end of the next month, I was notified that I was a finalist—they were serious… this was an honest interview process, not a fait accompli. Then they presented my name and credentials to the membership to vote on my candidacy. And, yes, they also did that background check.*

Character counts with this organization. And what was the effect of their comprehensive vetting process on me? Was I offended or put off by them checking up on me? Absolutely not. Rather, it made me understand that they believed in me and expected that I would give them my best effort.

Not only does character count regarding community perception, but it also counts in the boardroom. How members treat one another in the boardroom is crucial to creating the right atmosphere for productive discussion and decision-making. Members need to respect and trust one another, show integrity, and act maturely and responsibly. They should exude a commitment to and passion for the organization's cause, value service above self, and work collaboratively to fulfill the fiduciary duty of care.

*I was once called to facilitate a board retreat where some members felt the conduct of others on the board was disrespectful. Before the meeting, I interviewed all of the members. Regarding the concern for board member conduct, here is a sampling of the responses:*

*"We are a group that is critical of one another—raised voices, cutting off one another. I'd love to find a way for us to be more respectful of one another."*

*"We beat each other up. How do we respectfully communicate and be transparent without being harsh?"*

*"Sometimes my opinions get knocked down."*

*The first agenda item at the retreat was the projection of a slide on a big screen in the front of the room, listing these responses.*

*The room was quiet.*

*Whether embarrassed or chastened, the group unanimously agreed that nothing more needed to be said. The impact of openly sharing these perspectives with members during the retreat had a tremendously positive effect. The simple act of calling them out brought into sharp contrast the disconnect between how members believed they should act and the way they were actually interacting.*

*This led to a discussion about the difference between communication style and bad behavior. This discussion was a wonderful backdrop to the conclusion of the session, which was the identification of character attributes that the board embraced. The list included personal accountability, authentic engagement, integrity in words and actions, objectivity in decision-making, emotional maturity, "entrustability," and demonstration of ethical behavior.*

That session was several years ago. It was simple but transformative. To my knowledge, there hasn't been a significant incident of bad behavior in the boardroom since. They took this to heart. They made their expectations regarding character explicit and visible.

By interviewing prospective board members for character—validating it through research and interviewing references—and reinforcing expectations explicitly, you not only strengthen the cohesiveness of the board as a governance team but also insure the organization against disreputable behavior and bad press.

## Practical Exercise

Following are practices that will help you understand the character of prospective board members.

First, research your candidates. Google search, for example, gives us access to an extraordinary amount of information. I once conducted a search for a client and thought we had found the perfect candidate with the perfect experience. We did a thorough Google search—it took a bit of time as we cross-referenced several sources. But, we discovered that the individual had served time for misuse of company funds. Obviously, none of this appeared in the information the candidate provided!

Ask for and contact references. Though candidates likely recommend references that view them positively, it still is useful to hear what references have to say. Tell them that you want to make sure the candidate is the right fit. Tell them about the organization, the roles and responsibilities the individual will fulfill as a board member, and the challenges board members are likely to face. Ask what they believe the candidate can contribute. What skills and acumen do they bring to the board? Are there any unique attributes that make them a good fit? Then ask what they like about this person. And don't hesitate to ask if there are areas where they

think the candidate may benefit from the board's onboarding and education program.

Consider using a tool like the Hartman Value Profile. I use the Axiometrics version. If you go to www.jmuellerassociates.com, my website, I have several pages of information on the profile, but let me summarize:

It is named for Dr. Robert Hartman, who was a young philosopher living in Germany during the late 1930s. Because of his opposition to Hitler's regime, his life was in danger. With the help of some allies, he was able to secretly leave the country just before the war.

Once in the United States, he conducted his research while serving on the faculty of Vanderbilt and the University of Tennessee. Reflecting upon his experience in his native Germany, his most famous quote is: "If evil can be so efficiently organized, why not good?" That sentiment seemed to drive his research. He is known as the father of the field of axiology, which is concerned with valuing and the hierarchy of values. Through his research, he demonstrated that the values we hold determine how we think, feel, and act.

The Hartman Value Profile represents just one small aspect of Hartman's research. It was brought to life by Hartman's protégé and graduate student, Wayne Carpenter, after Hartman's untimely death at a rather early age. Over three decades, Carpenter ensured that the profile was developed as a reliable resource. That it was scientifically based in Hartman's research, peer-reviewed by academics at leading universities, and validated by psychometricians who were recognized experts in axiology. He created a tool that verifiably reveals peoples' thinking styles and how that impacts their ability to manage, provide customer service, be effective in sales, provide executive leadership, or their ability to be effective in a number of professions, from sports to medicine.

The Hartman Value Profile is designed with the user in mind. It is easy to access and takes about ten minutes to complete. Though a simple exercise, it is quite profound in what it can measure. For example, each part of the two-part exercise can measure 6.4 quadrillion permutations. The underlying mathematical and statistical framework built upon Hartman's research immediately analyzes the results. The Hartman Value Profile was field-tested for over thirty years before it was released to the market.

The profiling exercise can generate various individual reports depending upon the purpose. For example, an individual coaching report provides an analysis of one's strengths and hurdles and offers guidance on how one can improve one's abilities. The candidate interview guide provides a profile of the candidate's strengths and areas of development with interview questions to explore the fit with the organization.

I have used the profile for nearly three decades with organizations across the country, from small nonprofits to nationally recognized institutions. I highly recommend using this tool in recruiting board members. I also recommend using it first with your existing board and staff. When I have used this with organizations—whether the board, the staff or, best-case scenario, with both—it improves communication and strengthens esprit de corps. I have found that boards enjoy it because it provides clear insight and context for engaging discussion and, when recruiting, it provides a foundation for highly effective candidate interviews.

*Several years ago, a board chair called on me to confide that members of the board were questioning the character and integrity of staff members. They believed they were holding back information. He hoped that the staff members were not intentionally hiding things. Still, board members were consistently caught off guard by surprises.*

*This was a national nonprofit whose board members lived in states literally from coast to coast. The board convened four times each year for two days. The meetings were informative and engaging.*

*Here is how he described the issue to me. "We have our quarterly board meetings, and we discuss the issues and strategies with the senior members of the team. We have a plan of action to follow—to which both board and staff members agree. Then, within a few weeks, we begin to pick up bits and pieces of information from the staff that are inconsistent with what we thought we had agreed to. At the next board meeting, it's like we hadn't made any plans at all. We have to backpedal, and discussions get a little heated and defensive. Members of the board rightfully feel disrespected, having invested all this time and energy. We need to figure out what the heck is going on."*

*The members of the staff senior leadership team were at a loss. "We followed the plan, but a lot happens in three months. And when things change, sometimes we have to move quickly." A very valid statement given the scope of their work.*

*After interviewing the members of the board and the staff, I suggested we employ the Hartman Value Profile to look at how members of the board and staff process information. I would create a decision-making style map of both groups and see what it told us.*

The brilliance of Robert Hartman's approach (and thus the beauty of the Hartman Value Profile) is that it measures how we think. His research showed that every one of us processes (or thinks about) the world through three mental talents: (i) intrinsic thinking or empathy, (ii) extrinsic thinking or practical judgment, and (iii) systemic thinking or system judgment.

Intrinsic thinking or empathy is the non-time-bound, nonjudgmental immediate connection to people or things. Hartman showed that everyone can have a gut-sense or intuition immediately upon experiencing something. Everyone has the capability, but not everyone pays attention to it, has full access to it, or possesses sufficient clarity to use it effectively.

Extrinsic or practical thinking is what I call "present moment awareness." It is the ability to see and appreciate the practical, functional, and material value of things and thus make choices. For example, you engage in this thinking when choosing what to wear for a particular occasion or in a work setting, deciding whether Word or Excel is the best tool to use to create a team document. It is about understanding options, comparing them, and making choices about which best serves your needs. Again, everyone has the capability, though some have limitations.

Systemic thinking or system judgment is the ability to see and appreciate systems and order, and employs both conceptual and analytical thinking. This is the realm of the imagination where we conceive of ideas or models that guide our decision-making. As with intrinsic and extrinsic thinking, everyone has the capability, though some have limitations.

When we map a team, the thinking-style or decision-making culture is made explicit. The aggregate styles of all the team members create the thinking style map of the culture. And within that culture, there are even explicit style clusters that clarify how the team processes information and makes decisions.

So, what did we discover with this national nonprofit? Some extraordinarily interesting things immediately shed light on the problem.

As context, over the thirty years I have used this tool, I have seen a repeated pattern that people are drawn to people who think like they do. I'm not talking about politics, business, or even fashion preferences. It's more fundamental than that. We like to be around people who process information like we do. I have seen many teams evolve into groups that process information alike. It's naturally more comfortable to be around people who think the same way we do, and we are drawn to them in work settings.

*What we discovered was that the thinking-style of the board and the staff were almost exactly alike. But that does not mean conflict-free. In fact, that similarity of thinking created the conflict, and here is why (the following types are not mutually exclusive): twenty-four of the twenty-six members of the board and senior executives were creative, individualistic, inventive, or original thinkers. Sixteen were an unconventional, out-of-the-box type of thinkers. Seventeen were deliberative thinkers (prone to overthinking things), and a number of them were discrete (not sharing ideas) or skeptical (question others' ideas).*

*Because almost all of them were creative, individualistic, inventive, or original thinkers, at board meetings they could talk about ideas for hours or days, continually coming up with new approaches and concepts. This approach was reinforced by the majority of them being deliberative thinkers who enjoy poking and probing and considering all the various facets of an idea. And then there was a sprinkling of those who seldom shared their thoughts no matter how long the group deliberated (the discrete ones), along with the small group that questioned any idea that was put forward by someone else (the skeptics).*

*So, what was the root of the problem? The creative, individualistic, inventive, original thinking isn't confined to the boardroom. The senior management team authentically agreed to the decisions of the board, but they didn't stop thinking when the board meeting ended. Their creative instincts continued to operate, and ideas naturally morphed as challenges arose. They truly believed that their line of thinking was consistent with the board's decisions, even as it evolved. They were not conscious of the fact that the board members were not experiencing their daily challenges, thus unaware of the factors that brought about the changes to the plan.*

*When I shared this map at the board meeting, there was a huge sense of relief, and self-effacing laughter as those in the room recognized their styles and their collusion in creating the problem. This resolved the board's concern about the character of the staff.*

*The solution, though simple, was tough to sustain. It was decided that the CEO would provide weekly topline updates to the board regarding progress and changes that were relevant to the decisions made at the board meeting. It was difficult to maintain a cadence of reporting, and it required reminders from the board chair. But, the most important advancement was the board now understood the source of the problem and could address it directly.*

Using the Hartman Value Profile with your board will help you understand how the new candidates fit with the existing thinking style and intentional culture of the board. You can actually strengthen the capacity of your board by consciously introducing different thinking styles through the candidates you recruit. Each style has a unique way of processing information and offers unique perspectives. When approached intentionally and when thoughtfully managed, the benefits are enhanced.

One last comment about tools like the Hartman Value Profile when they are used to build nonprofit capacity. Because the Hartman Value Profile objectively assesses job-related skills and traits, using it makes recruitment decisions more defensible by adding an extra layer of objectivity to the process. Organizations that use validated testing programs in accordance with legal guidelines are better prepared to defend these procedures should someone challenge their practices.

A common misconception with recruitment evaluation is that using such tools increases legal exposure or somehow leads to additional legal risk. The opposite is true when using a validated tool like the Hartman Value Profile because it is objective and thus mitigates against interviewer bias. In Chapters 4 and 5, I dig deeply into the deceptive nature of unconscious bias—which we all possess. Using a tool like the Hartman Value Profile cuts through the bias interviewers may bring to decision-making. It provides an unbiased objective assessment.

*I had an experience recently with a client that supports this approach. In reviewing final candidates for a deputy director, the CEO had eliminated a highly qualified candidate with strong character from consideration because he had interacted with her in another setting and concluded that she wasn't a fit. I suggested that we employ the Hartman Value Profile to see what shows up. After reviewing the results, the CEO admitted he recognized his decision was influenced by a personal bias. He then invited the candidate for an interview. After background check and other due diligence, he offered her the job. She proved to be a perfect fit.*

In an era when we are beginning to recognize the extraordinary impact of bias on society, a tool like the Hartman Value Profile is a very valuable asset to employ.

When you get to the interview stage, ask candidates to describe their personal values. Ask how they have handled conflict—particularly on other boards where they have served. Explain that sometimes discussions can be intense and ask candidates how they deal with difficult people in those situations.

Conduct a background check on the finalists. We often hesitate to interview with this level of scrutiny because it may make us feel uncomfortable... but it is less uncomfortable than having to deal with a difficult personality, meeting after meeting or, possibly, a public embarrassment later on.

Do I hear you saying, "this is a bit much!"? I respect the skepticism and the discomfort. But why would anyone fill the highest office in their organization without careful attention to recruiting the candidates best suited to the responsibility? Often we undervalue the importance of governance roles... then we have to live with the results. I have seen the harmful effects of board members whose character is not consistent with the values of the organization.

# Term Limits

Great boards make sure that the right people are in the seats around the boardroom table and that those people have a firm grasp of their responsibilities. Once someone is sitting in that chair in the boardroom, the course has been set for that person's term of service. What do I mean by this? Over the last forty years of working with boards, I can count on one hand the number of times I have seen ineffective or difficult board members gracefully separate from a board. Removing a board member is risky and potentially embarrassing, and I have not encountered even one board chair who is comfortable with the task. This is one reason I recommend terms of service. If nothing else, it ensures that ineffective and difficult board members can be termed off.

This is a topic that I have debated with a number of governing boards because term limits have both benefits and challenges.

## *The Benefits*

By changing board composition, the organization is better able to adapt to changing needs. As organizations and the communities they serve evolve, recruiting individuals with new perspectives and skill sets help an organization sustain its relevance and respond effectively.

Second, term limits improve the likelihood of attracting busy, productive people. Limited terms are often more attractive to this type of person; as opposed to a perpetual commitment that requires them to resign if they want to end their service on the board.

Third, strategic recruitment. Managing board composition provides the impetus to think about recruitment strategically and for the long term. It provides the opportunity to step back and really think about what you need in terms of character, competence, connections, and culture.

Fourth, term limits help prevent stagnation and bias. Without regular infusion of new members, boards may lose the ability to see issues from fresh perspectives, so organizational innovation and growth may suffer.

Fifth, and we will address this in detail in the chapter on composition, term limits help nonprofit boards maintain diversity and balance. They provide a consistent opportunity for the board to recruit people with diverse or underrepresented points of view.

Last, as I mentioned above, term limits allow boards to release members who are not suited to the responsibilities of governance. From the non-engaged board members' perspective, term limits allow them to politely cycle off without embarrassment.

## The Challenges

For starters, continuously recruiting new board members requires significant time and effort to properly onboard and orient them to the board and the organization.

Another challenge is continuity and planning. New board members need to be educated, to be brought up to speed, so the board must manage this transition and address gaps in understanding and perspective.

There is also loss of history, expertise, and knowledge. As seasoned members leave, the board loses the richness of their experience. So, the board needs to have mechanisms to continue to engage board members who cycle off, to be able to access their wisdom and intelligence.

And there is disruption. Changes in board composition disrupt the rhythm, flow, and comfort that develop when people work together over time. So, efficiency and productivity may lag.

When you consider both the benefits and challenges of board term limits, the benefits far outweigh the challenges. Each of these challenges can be managed with a little forethought and creativity.

Even when a board has term limits, careful vetting of candidates remains critical. Don't get caught in the trap of thinking you can change disruptive or difficult behavior. We carry on in life in a way that has evolved from childhood through our life experiences. Unless we encounter a crisis or experience an epiphany, most of us will not change. And the older we get, the less malleable we tend to be. I am not saying this is true for everyone. But, generally speaking, as a rule, you can rely on it. As a therapist once told me decades ago, "don't expect people to be what you hope, expect them to be consistent."

## Practical Exercise

Following are a few core questions to use to guide a conversation with any prospective candidate. Feel free to add to the list. Though the questions may change in form from person to person, by the end of the conversation, you are likely to have a good handle on the person's character.

• What are you passionate about in life?

• How do your friends describe you? What do they say are your best attributes? What do they find challenging?

• How do you describe your values?

• Why do you volunteer?

• What about our organization makes you interested in us?

• In your mind, what is the most important thing we do for the community?

• Why do you want to serve our board?

• Sometimes board discussions can get heated. How do you respond when you find your opinions to be in conflict with another board member?

• What values or personal characteristics would you want your fellow board members to possess?

• What do you expect from fellow board members when you serve on a board?

# CHAPTER 3

# Competence

**C**ompetence: *the mastery of knowledge and skills that enables one to possess deep understanding and consistently deliver high-quality results.*

I volunteer to serve on nonprofit boards and help fundraise. I believe that I need to experience the roles and responsibilities about which I am asked to consult. Most often, it is a gratifying experience.

But not always.

*Several years ago, while serving on the board of a national advocacy organization, I recruited a lawyer/investor active in the LGBTQ community. She was an Ivy League graduate and a sound thinker. She brought a deeply informed perspective from the LGBTQ community that would enhance the organization's ability to serve its constituency. Bringing her on board was like taking a bright light into a dim room—she could see things others could not.*

*She called me shortly after her first board meeting to say she was resigning. When I tried to persuade her to stick with it for a few months, she adamantly said no.*

*The LGBTQ community was a critical constituency of the mission of this organization, and, she said, they don't even recognize that we are part of it.*

*I couldn't disagree.*

*I had misjudged the board's and the CEO's readiness to have this individual on the team. They were in "credential" mode and, heck, she was a lawyer, wasn't she? But that's not what she brought. She was not a practicing attorney but rather had been a successful CEO and investment manager, and she had successfully chaired a prominent LGBTQ organization in a major metropolitan area. But because the board was not looking for competence, only credentials, they could not understand the value she brought to the board.*

There is a huge difference between competence and a credential. A credential is a certification of sorts for which an individual has successfully completed training or course work in some intellectual or skill pursuit. The value of that credential is dependent upon the credentialing agency, its reputation, and the rigor of the course work. So, a credential on its own is not evidence of competence. By contrast, competence is *the mastery of knowledge and skills that enables one to possess deep understanding and consistently deliver high-quality results.* Competence is assessed by an individual's performance and success in the field of one's endeavors.

*This board was suffering from a common ailment of governance. Board members were oblivious to a range of governance responsibilities and opportunities. I use oblivious because their state of thinking was more than being unaware. Instead, it's a case of not being able to see something or respond to something because it simply does not occur to them—it's outside their frame of reference.*

*Board members were not only oblivious to the responsibility to serve nontraditional audiences, but they were oblivious to the opportunity staring them squarely in the face: a board member with competencies that would have had a transformative effect on programs and the ability of the organization to fulfill its mission—by serving a new audience hungry for its support.*

What do we do when a board is clueless about the competencies it needs to thrive?

First, board members must be receptive, as we discussed earlier. Whenever I'm called in, I start by talking to board members individually, asking questions about what they see as the value of the organization, what hopes they have for it, what challenges the organization is facing, how they view the role of the board and responsibilities of members. These simple questions give me a clear sense of each member's perspective: the way they see their role, the breadth of their thinking, their governance acumen, their reasons for being involved, and how they view problems and opportunities.

To bring about change, not everyone has to be ready, but there is a need for a few influential champions who are ready, in order to achieve a shift. When I shared this with a friend, he told me, "This concept has been described as 'the critical mass' of influencers rubric. Critical mass is estimated by taking the square root of any number. For instance, on a board consisting of twenty-five members, it will take about five key influencers to carry the day. Not a bad rule of thumb." I agree.

Nevertheless, I've had success with an organization when only three out of eighteen board members were ready—but they were the right three. They had the courage, character, and acumen to catalyze change. It took a while, and we started carefully, but because these three grasped the importance of the need for change, they were… how can I best describe them… "politely relentless." When such individuals are not in place, attempts to bring about change will not get traction, and research shows that it can actually result in deeper entrenchment in current beliefs and behaviors.

There are ways to use a skilled consultant to "shake things up and wake things up." But that requires careful pre-engagement work. To get people to move to a new place, you have to help them see it in their imagination—or as I wrote in an earlier chapter, elasticity of imagination. The tension that I carefully watch when leading organizations through change is how flexible they are in their thinking. How far can I stretch their imagination without snapping the connection to their current comfort zone? So, I work at building a compelling view of the new world that is rooted in their beliefs and values. Because I have had meaningful conversations with each member, I know what is important to each of them. The language I use in constructing this new place is the language that they have used in describing their point of view. By doing so, I reinforce the vibrancy of their feelings and trust in the new idea. The stronger the connection to their world view, the more I can pull them toward the new idea. If they lose faith, the connection I've created will snap, and they will be more entrenched in their old ideas.

Underlying this process is trust, which I have to win by being credible, reliable, trustworthy, and completely invested in their best interests.

Let's say the board has bought in and is ready for change. The process is simple to describe: step back, unplug, and reboot. *Step back* to the fundamentals upon which the organization is built, *unplug* all assumptions, and *reboot* from a fresh perspective.

A few years later, the national advocacy board was able to engage in the process I just described, but it needed to wait until a dynamic leader took the reins. An individual I recruited just as I was leaving the board.

On a brighter note, I was fortunate to help another organization achieve a completely different outcome. In the middle of a board meeting, as members of the board were reviewing a list of board member applicants, everyone was redlining the applications and highlighting work experience and educational credentials. They turned to me and asked, "Jim, what do you think?" My response was something like, "If you look around the room, you see all sorts of credentials. But what attributes do you notice in the most effective members, and what competencies do you need to develop?"

This was a golden opportunity that paid off for the organization. It was the perfect moment to change the direction of the organization through one simple question.

I had been working with the board for a few years, and they immediately recognized the value of the question. They also recognized that the answers weren't found in the applications or the resumes. They needed to step back, identify the competencies they valued, and interview promising candidates.

It is so vital for boards to genuinely examine the competencies they need to become the organization they envision—to grow, adapt, and strengthen their leadership and their programs. By thoughtfully engaging in this exercise, boards open themselves to considering some intangibles that aren't immediately evident upon meeting a person but can be discovered. These include characteristics such as deliberative thinking, sound judgment, emotional maturity, a good sense of humor, proactive conflict management skills, for example. Boards should not just look at the typical skill sets to strengthen the governing body. There is much more to consider.

By contrast with the governing board in my first example, the ensuing conversation with this board had an immediate impact. It was part of a cascade of change that has transformed the organization, raising it to a new level of performance.

As in the first example, when assessing its members' governance competence, boards often look at credentials—we need a lawyer, or an accountant, or a marketer, or a political or civic leader—rather than looking deeper at whether the individual is competent in knowledge and abilities that the board needs to thrive. Just because someone works in a particular profession doesn't mean they are good at it or possess competencies the board needs.

Yes, organizations need individuals competent in their professions to assist the organization. But do these individuals need to serve on the board to volunteer their services? Too often, boards defer to getting free professional advice through board members.

This isn't necessarily a problem, and if they are competent, there can be a great advantage. But great governance requires members to possess a particular set of competencies beyond business acumen—competencies that are often overlooked. When board members lack these competencies, it significantly diminishes their contribution.

What are the critical competencies a board needs its members to possess to thrive? On the top of my list is effective deliberation. The various components related to effective deliberation include intellect, communication (especially the ability to actively listen), sound judgment, governance aptitude, sense of humor, patience, knowledge, subject-matter expertise related to the organization's programs, and insight. Though not a comprehensive list, these are some of the fundamentals. Each board has different needs at different times. The highest-functioning boards make time annually to identify critical competencies and carefully define them before recruiting new members.

Let's look at some of the competencies I noted above: intellect, communication (including active listening), sound judgment, governance aptitude, sense of humor, patience, knowledge, and subject-matter expertise related to the organization's cause.

## Intellect

We are all familiar with IQ and, more recently, EQ—emotional quotient, aka emotional intelligence. However, Thomas Chamorro-Premuzic, professor of business psychology at University College London, suggests that we also need to consider CQ, curiosity quotient. In balancing a board's deliberative ability, I believe a board should look for all three.

IQ is basic brainpower, the capacity to handle "high cognitive load" and retain information. These are the people that can hold many divergent bits of information in their minds, see solutions, and provide sound rationales.

EQ refers to a person's emotional aptitude, the ability to perceive, control, and express emotions. High EQ people are adaptable and able to navigate stressful, complex, and uncertain environments. These individuals have a tendency toward entrepreneurialism and innovation.

The CQ folks have hungry minds; they are inquisitive, counterconformist, and tolerant of ambiguity. They tend to be nuanced, subtle thinkers that produce simple solutions for complex problems.

Think about your board. Which of these thinking styles could benefit your board? Do any or many of your board members possess them? There is an inherent conflict in mixing these styles. For example, those with a high IQ may tend toward structured, analytical thinking. While those more in the EQ realm will tend to lean toward adapting to others' needs and interests. And the CQ thinkers tend to be a bit disruptive, less concerned about order, more concerned with finding a satisfying unique solution.

Though each of us has access to intelligence, empathy, and creativity, we tend to gravitate toward one or the other as we think and process. There is a real benefit to striking a balance that embraces all three styles. But to succeed, it takes intentional and informed practices that encourage and manage these diverse styles. Board members need to understand what these different approaches to problem-solving contribute to effective decision-making, and through cooperative dialog, distill the best solutions. Managing this process effectively is the responsibility of everyone, but particularly the board chair, who needs to be an effective mediator.

# Communication

Communication is the most common challenge facing boards for several reasons—which is why it is critically important to get this right before and during the recruitment process. The most common cause is conflict in communication *style*—when and how we communicate. Some are quiet, some are loud and assertive. Some are articulate, some struggle to find words. Some listen, some don't. All make assumptions that they are understood—most think they are right... Sometimes I wonder how we communicate at all.

Let's take another look at the example I raised in Chapter 1 regarding the board member who resigned because she was a "cultural misfit." As you may recall, one of the board chair's concerns was communication. And it wasn't limited to the board; he was concerned that the senior management team was not being transparent with the board. Using the Hartman Value Profile, we diagnosed the source of the communication problem—or more accurately, we revealed the dynamics that made communication a particular challenge.

What we discovered was a style of thinking predominant among members of the board and the senior team. The core attributes of this style of thinking are creativity, individuality, flexibility, originality, and skepticism. This style of thinking made the organization effective in its advocacy work because it was nimble and responsive to changes in the environment—and thus, the organization was never backed into a corner, and the leadership always adapted and developed new approaches.

Nevertheless, embedded in this strength was the organization's communication problem—the decision-making landscape was in constant flux with new ideas arising quickly and being implemented with the same speed. While there was no intent to hide anything, without communication structures or policies in place, communication wasn't keeping pace with decision-making; the team was not transparent and was not fulfilling its obligation to keep the board informed.

Here, policies and procedures were insufficient because, as Peter Drucker is attributed with saying, "culture eats strategy for breakfast." Communication style, like any other personal attribute, is developed over time and is intimately linked to how you process and make sense of the world. Telling someone to communicate better, or to follow new procedures that do not come naturally to them, requires more than instruction. It requires sound *rationale* (why it's important), *awareness* of its importance (why for everyone—not just your colleagues), and a cadence of *accountability* (did you do what you said you'd do).

In this case, it worked—and it is important to note that it worked because of the foresight and insight of the board chair, who recognized the need and championed the process.

*The chair set aside an entire morning of the quarterly board meeting to discuss the issue, identify a strategy, and secure buy-in. I shared the results of the Hartman Value Profile. I explained that no one was at fault, that no one was intentionally hiding anything. I then facilitated a discovery session with the board and senior staff to craft practices and policies that worked uniquely for this organization: frequent, to the point, brief communiques that everyone agreed to read. That simple practice was transformative. Sustaining it required attention to accountability. The simple mantra at each board meeting: Did you write what/when/how you said you would? Did you read what others wrote? Did you respond promptly?*

As with any of these practices, this isn't a one-time fix. As new people join the organization and others leave, you lose a bit of memory—along with some effective practices. Also, as people transition, the culture and style of the organization change. It is crucial to stay vigilant and aware as the organization grows and evolves, to stay ahead of things that might cause problems and act as needed to fix them.

What does this have to do with recruitment and onboarding? First, it is important to understand how and how well prospective new board members communicate. Also, it is important to discuss the organization's communication challenges and approaches so that every new member is well-informed. Several organizations with which I consult use the Hartman Value Profile in all of their recruitment efforts—members of board and staff—and many of those do annual checkups, a fun exercise that reveals the various styles of members and how to integrate everyone's style into an effective team dynamic.

## Sound Judgment

*The CEO of a large nonprofit organization came to me because he was concerned about the compensation package that was given to the founder upon her retirement. Since the founder had invested her life in the organization for over three decades, with little compensation and no retirement—and was now facing health issues—the board created a consultation agreement. It paid the founder an annual consulting fee that was six figures. But there were no reporting requirements and no defined scope of work. Making things worse, the founder still served as a voting member on the board.*

Good intentions, bad judgment.

*With the sound advice of a labor attorney, who was a former IRS employee, the CEO and I were able to convince the board of the problem, particularly the penalties the organization might face if audited. The founder immediately resigned from the board, the levels of compensation were adjusted to reflect marketplace realities, and a scope of work was crafted that directly reflected the current activities of the founder.*

Sound judgment is a concept you think you understand until you try to describe it. The tricky thing about sound judgment is that it is rooted in the decision-maker's beliefs and values—what you believe is right and wrong or good and bad. In matters of religion and politics, for example, there is little common ground on sound judgment. I know this for a fact. Just ask my brother or sister whether I am capable of sound judgment when we talk about those two topics—and because I use sound judgment, I avoid raising those topics with them.

Sound judgment is a critical component of good governance. In the boardroom, sound judgment is the ability to *fully grasp the issue at hand*—to perceive and appreciate the implications and nuance and to understand the context of the issue. It is the ability to know why an issue is an *issue* and how it came onto the table for discussion, and then to *make decisions that are in the organization's best interest.*

In my opening vignette, the CEO exercised sound judgment. By seeking counsel and delivering the recommendations to the board regarding how to restructure good intentions into legal compliance, he put the organization on safe ground. The timing was fortuitous because a year later, a disgruntled terminated employee contacted the IRS claiming the organization was operating illegally, which prompted an audit. Because of the memo to the file and the change in practice, the organization was protected by IRS' Rebuttable Presumption of Reasonableness rule. The only changes that resulted from the audit were reclassifying a few positions to non-exempt.

When recruiting new board members, assess their ability to use sound judgment. Do this by employing carefully structured interview questions that probe the individual's decision-making process.

## Governance Aptitude

*I was contacted by a board member of a national association who was heading up the strategic planning process. He was concerned that the board was too invested in organizational management. This was clearly evidenced in their board structure. There was a vice-president for programs, a vice-president for education, a vice-president for management, and a former board member (also a professional in the field) was the lone staff member.*

*Though the organization was decades old, the structure was almost the same as the day it was founded—when it was all-volunteer run… and everyone was completely invested in the importance of their roles. With board members working at the grassroots, no one was looking to the horizon and guiding the ship—and the nature of the profession served by the association had dramatically shifted since its founding. As a result, the organization became insular, with board members invested in maintaining their "jobs" and guiding the association into a posture of "defending the profession and its professionals" rather than stepping back to gain a broader view, to recognize where the "profession" they were defending might be losing relevance. Market conditions and boundary definitions were changing. They were not seeing the threats and opportunities in the broader evolving environment.*

Governance's primary fiduciary responsibility is oversight, which requires board members to guide the organization to stay relevant to the communities it serves. Though this includes holding management accountable for outcomes—it must be done without meddling in management, which caused the organization I just described to lose sight of its larger responsibility.

In simple terms, governance is responsible for "what" the organization does, and the management team is responsible for "how" the organization does it. When governance becomes enmeshed in management, it loses its ability to perform its most crucial governance function—oversight, because the line between oversight and management has vanished. I have seen boards destructively disrupt the functioning of an organization because they cross that line. It is a line that should never be crossed.

Governance is akin to navigating a large ship—that of being always attuned to the larger seascape, being vigilant for icebergs in the north and reefs in the south, providing guidance, and raising a red flag when necessary. Governance's only management responsibility is to partner with the CEO, to actively engage the CEO, and to hire or fire the CEO.

Those who are highly competent at governance invest time and energy cultivating a strong working relationship with the CEO. They use finesse, ask good questions to clarify meaning and reveal intentions, and possess insight into the motives of other members of the board and of the management team—while respecting other individuals' professional acumen.

Back to our story:

*It took a few years to change habits and wean board members off their management tasks, but one key to success was identifying and recruiting new board members who possessed governance aptitude. These were individuals who not only understood the responsibilities of governance but also possessed the fortitude to hold fast to its principles. Over the next few years, through education and strategic recruitment, they have transformed the organization—rewriting its vision, mission, and value proposition, and shifting its focus to include a broad range of professionals who are becoming avid members. They hired professionally trained association management executives to the staff. Membership is growing, and the organization is thriving.*

## Sense of Humor

Why humor? Because it makes us laugh. And laughter is healthy! It strengthens our immune system, boosts our mood, diminishes our pain, and protects us from the harmful effects of stress. It lightens our burdens, opens our hearts, inspires hope, connects us to others, and keeps us grounded, focused, and alert.

I remember once when the late Jim Lehrer, PBS NewsHour anchor, looked at the camera and said: "Three guys walked into a bar... the fourth one ducked." Deadpan, straight-faced. That day the news wasn't so bad... mostly because I kept chuckling. (And, yes, I recognize it's a dad joke.)

Have you ever noticed that, once you laugh, how much more easily you release anger and forgive?

Laughter opens us up to see the absurdity of our self-importance—and that of others. Too often we get too serious—as if these little inconveniences and minor offenses mean anything. Have you ever sat in a room with people who take themselves too seriously? It's god-awful. As a friend said, "humor helps us take our work seriously, not ourselves."

To elicit laughter, you don't have to be a lively sprite or a comedian. Some of the funniest people I know are the quietest. But they come out with a simple remark at the right moment that sends the people in the room into a fit of laughter that puts everyone at ease.

When I talk to boards about recruitment, I always recommend that they interview candidates for their sense of humor—among other essential attributes. Is the person playful, light, or fun to be around? When you get to the most challenging issues of governance, when there are deep divides in opinion, or when passions run high... it's important to laugh.

## Patience

It is hard for me to be patient. I meditate, use relaxation exercises, practice active listening, and have even tried biofeedback. All of these have been helpful, but even as a little kid, it was hard for me to sit still.

If you happen to struggle with attention deficit or hyperactivity disorder, I'm with you. It's hard work for us to be patient and present, but it is so crucial in the governance setting. It's kind of like being married; if you want to be heard and happy, listen first. One day my daughter, who was seventeen, came into my office speaking in a loud voice. I said, *stop yelling.* She said, *dad, you told me why people yell… because you're not listening.* I guess she actually hears what I say! I took my own advice, shut up, and listened… she stopped yelling because I heard her.

One of my great lessons in patience was watching a friend steer an organization onto the right course. It took over three years. Clearly, it wasn't a job suited to me, but, even so, I learned from his example of patience. He understood that we can't force people to change, but if we hold fast to the vision and listen to fellow board members as they learn and process, over time the results will come.

We can also express patience in the little moments when we just take a breath and listen to our governance colleagues. When we do this, others experience our patience as respect and as caring enough to listen—even if we disagree.

When recruiting members to your board, do they listen in the interview? Do they rush through the conversation, or are they present with you? Do they let you complete your thoughts?

Do they ask clarifying questions? A dear friend, who is a former business school president, shared with me the acronym, WAIT, "Why am I talking?" He told me it was a life-saver for him: "I find WAIT is especially useful after I've asked a question. Stop talking. Listen, really listen for the answer. It also reminds me that when I do speak, I ought to confirm my purpose before launching into a spiel."

Patience is a virtue.

## Knowledge

To be effective for your board, what do prospective members need to know? Does your organization occupy a specialty niche affected by government regulations? Do you work in other countries so that you are affected by international law? Do you deal with highly confidential information that affects the safety of your clientele? Do you have highly complex program contracts and unique funding sources? Do you have agreements with other charitable organizations that entail financial obligations and performance expectations? Do you work across socio-economic communities, solving complex social problems?

Every charitable organization operates within a unique set of circumstances that requires board members to possess sufficient knowledge to govern effectively. When building your recruitment profile, it is important to reflect upon what knowledge prospective members need to have to be effective. What professional, social, civic, or other experiences would imbue them with an understanding of how the world works that would be most helpful in governance?

*An example of the value of board members with the right knowledge is the foundation board I chaired that serves the needs of a community-based school for the arts. Our board consisted of parents, teachers, the chair of the PTA, and the principal as ex-officio. These individuals were very knowledgeable about the issues that our mission addressed, so our funding decisions were very well-informed. The board also served an important function we never intended. It became a place where a group of highly informed and competent decision-makers discussed issues that arose among parents, the community, the school board, and the school itself. While keeping appropriate confidences, the principal would use our group as a sounding board regarding various challenges she was facing. We were also able to be a voice in the community to champion important issues while sidestepping the politics.*

Though every board member needs to be oriented and informed during the onboarding process, your recruitment process will be much more effective if you start by screening for prospective members' knowledge of your mission, your programs, and generally about how things work in your world.

But, as in all things, be mindful of balance and intention. There is a difference between someone knowledgeable and someone knowledgeable who has a personal agenda. In a later chapter, I will share a story that demonstrates how a single individual with selfish intentions can be disruptive and damage a board's effectiveness. As I discussed in Chapter 2, character counts. So, when you recruit for knowledge, keep character in mind.

## Subject-Matter Expertise

An extension of knowledge is subject-matter expertise. I'm not talking about particular business acumens, such as finance or marketing. I'm talking about specific subject-matter expertise that can improve your governance ability. Though it is critically important to draw a clear line between governance and management—we should never confuse the two—someone with particular subject-matter expertise can improve the board's ability to make decisions.

For example, if your organization deals with homelessness, who would possess subject-matter expertise? First and foremost, someone who has experienced homelessness. Or if you deal with spousal abuse, possibly a professional who is well versed in the field—someone who possesses knowledge of policy, proven practices, or important nuances that can lend expertise in planning and decision-making.

Since a primary function of governance is setting policy, carefully selecting prospective board members with specific subject-matter expertise can enhance the board's ability to make sound decisions. How one manages the input of these individuals once they are on the board is an important issue, but is beyond the scope of this book. As we saw in the example of our hi-tech executive in chapter 1 who resigned within the first year of service, it takes finesse and skill to achieve a balance that demonstrates receptivity and good judgment.

## Practical Exercise:

Following are few core questions to use to guide a conversation with any prospective candidate. Feel free to add to the list. Though the questions may change in form from person to person, by the end of the conversation, you are likely to have a good handle on the person's competence.

- Tell me a little about your board experience.
- How have you been effective on the boards where you served?
- What would others who served with you describe as your strengths?
- In your opinion, what are the core responsibilities of board members?
- What do you hope to bring to our board, in terms of your personal skills and abilities?
- What is your experience with financial and legal documents and compliance issues?
- In the boardroom, how do you interact effectively with a difficult personality? What skills to you call upon?
- Generally speaking, what do you need to know about an issue to make an informed decision?
- How do you assess whether the board has made a good decision?

# CHAPTER 4

# Connections

Connections: *relationships in which people are linked to or associated with others.*

*As I wrote earlier, I served on the board of a foundation that supported arts education for a community school where 80 percent of the students were on subsidized meals. The beauty of the school being both a community-based school and an arts school was experienced through the art that all the children created and shared, whether music, drama, dance, or digital and visual art. Each child's artistic expression transcended language and cultural barriers, as many of the children came from homes where English was not the primary language.*

*When I joined the board, the organization was about five years old, but floundering, not raising money. I discovered that the membership was populated by public figures who liked the accolades, a junior bank executive who was looking for parents to sign up for checking and savings accounts, a mystery man I never met who just liked being on the board, and some students' parents. After the first year, they asked me to chair the board.*

*Being the parent of a former student, I felt strongly about the power and importance of the school for the community and the students it served. I hesitated to serve as chair because I was well aware of the challenges. But I was also excited to take on the responsibility because I knew what was possible, and the rest of the board members were longing for leadership.*

Where does one start when governance is at a low ebb? What is the first thing to do?

*First on the list was achieving a clarity of purpose that resonates with the students' and schoolteachers' needs—and in a larger sense, one that resonated with the community. But before we could connect to the community, we needed to become crystal clear about who we were.*

Often, when their organizations are floundering, nonprofit leaders assume that "we just need more visibility." However, without a clear sense of identity and the language to describe it, you cannot connect to the broader community. Visibility is not what organizations need. Instead, they need to build a band of believers.

*We focused on the fundamentals of values, vision, mission, value proposition, and funding priorities. Some board members questioned the need to spend hours clarifying these statements.*

As I have learned through using the Hartman Value Profile, which can identify quadrillions of processing differences, everybody is different. Each of us has a different approach to processing information, expressing meaning, and making decisions. Some people immerse themselves in the minutiae, and others just want the bold facts.

Still, when it comes to articulating an organization's identity in a manner that truly conveys its essence so that people "get it" when they "see it," it's worth a bit of immersion in the minutiae—though be careful not to niggle.

For example, when you read the section in this book on core values, you will notice that I emphasize using one word for each core value, preferably a noun, as the starting place. I also recommend using only three or four core values. To arrive at three or four key words that describe the essence of your organization's identity takes time, debate, give-and-take, and careful choices.

It takes deliberative thoughtfulness to arrive at a true expression of your organization's identity. Early on in my practice, I would hand out a few pages of core value words to stimulate creative juices. To my chagrin, I discovered that most people would circle a few and proclaim, "that's us!" The result was a generic set of values that could apply to many different organizations.

The good stuff comes out at the moment people get frustrated and maybe a little agitated, and great debate ensues. People will aver for a position, and someone will challenge or suggest an alternate view. This is an important process.

Several decades ago, Sam Kaner captured this process in his "Facilitating Sustainable Agreements" model. To effectively grapple with these most important concepts and issues, you have to be willing to move into what he called "The Groan Zone." First, you have to move past your immediate assumptions and the thoughts that come easily to you into a space of divergent thinking. To do this, you must withhold making instant judgments and decide to just listen to others' points of view. This can be really tough for those who are wired for action.

As you move into the process, you will discover competing frames of reference. That is, your underlying assumptions and biases become a little more apparent to you and others in the room. At this moment you enter the highly uncomfortable "groan zone."

There is great value in achieving this stage in the conversation because you become open to new ways of thinking about things, you look at ideas for their own merit. As you enter this phase, you begin to develop a new framework of understanding that is shared with others in the conversation. That is, you see others' points of view, and you relinquish your tenacious hold to a framework that is outmoded or insufficient. You become receptive to learning something new, or you might change or freshen up your perspective in light of the other perspectives being offered. This is when you are ready to make really good choices. You synthesize your ideas with others and create statements that represent a new, valid and valuable, shared understanding.

*So, you can imagine what our discussions were like. Some board members were all in, some decided not to attend these planning meetings. But we maintained a quorum and enjoyed some profound and meaningful conversations about our purpose and identity. The payoff came when board members started talking to their friends or speaking out in the community. For the first time, members had the language to describe the work of the foundation and found it easier and even more pleasant to talk about its work.*

*Next, we tackled the challenge of getting more connected to the community. We discussed the importance of identifying prospective board members and other "community connectors" who were able and willing (willingness is critically important) to help the organization succeed in its mission. When board members asked why or "what do you mean," I explained, "we are afloat in our own little pond. Few people outside this room know that we exist; fewer know why we exist."*

It's the same thing with most charitable organizations. There are so many out there. Awareness alone just doesn't cut it anymore. You need to engage people in purposeful dialog, so they *really* understand not only your mission but the importance of what you are doing for their community and the expectations you have for their participation. And to achieve this, you must have the right messengers interpreting your mission and vision to prospective constituents. Thus, it is vital to identify people with the influence and the right connections in the community.

Even faced with this challenge, most board members just reach out to the people they like, or the ones that they feel have great reputations or those with whom they would like to be considered peers. But, to really serve a community, connections need to be strategic and intentional. The right connections within and across the community are vital to an organization's ability to succeed in its mission.

But, how do you break through this tendency to just look for people with whom you feel comfortable or those you admire?

We all make assumptions based on first impressions. Scientifically it's called implicit bias or implicit social cognition. We develop these biases because our brains process extraordinarily large amounts of information and complexities that life throws at us every moment. We create short cuts, mental categories that we use to quickly sort things. The result is that we fall prey to unconscious bias, for example, associating certain visual cues with value or character. Whether it's the clothes a person wears or the color or shape of someone's face, we make biased value judgments.

We develop these biases, or you might call them stereotypes, based upon our experiences in life and things we have been taught. They function unconsciously for the most part, and we aren't aware of the rational flaws because we don't examine them, we just accept them. The only time we change is when our thought patterns have created a real problem for us, or a good friend is courageous enough to bring them to our attention.

Our biases are triggered unconsciously and without our awareness or conscious control. They evoke feelings and attitudes about people based solely on their appearance, as I said, their voice, or even the color of their skin. In today's feeding-frenzied media environment, these biases are provoked and reinforced every minute of the day.

The sad news is that there is no solid evidence that diversity and awareness training ultimately impacts our implicit bias. But as board members, there is something that we can do about it.

The first step is to consider to whom your organization needs to be connected. Once you create a descriptive template or profile, you immediately take a step in the right direction away from your implicit biases because you are describing measurable attributes. I highly recommend four categories for connections:

1. Those you serve
2. Those who are influential in the community
3. Those who are affluent philanthropists and love your cause
4. Those equipped to help your organization better succeed at its mission and serve its community

As a reminder, connections are subsidiary to governance competence, which we addressed in an earlier chapter. Just because someone fits a category does not qualify that person for a board seat. Each individual recruited needs to be capable of governing.

*Category 1:* Those you serve. Among those you serve, who possesses governance competence, or can bring insights to the board regarding the people it serves? What qualities should they possess? What experiences should they have had that will help the board understand the needs of those it serves? Are there age, gender, or other personal attributes that should be considered in making a selection? The reason to recruit a person who connects you to the people you serve is that it enables you to serve them better. But, don't make this a token selection.

*One of our firm's clients is dedicated to including members of the community it serves on its board. These are individuals diagnosed with mental disabilities.*

You might say to me, "you just broke rule #1, competence to govern." If that has occurred to you, then please read the next chapter very carefully, because this thought is a clear indicator of an unconscious bias—either an implicit bias or a social categorization. Both of these are addressed in detail in the next chapter.

*When I have attended the client's board meetings, I notice that the community representatives tend to be quiet and a bit shy. But a few things occur because they are present. First, other board members don't treat them as different. They engage them as full partners in governance. An uninformed observer would have no indication that anything is different about them. Second, they keep the board grounded in reality. At every meeting, the cause that the organization serves sits at the table. And third, they offer an extraordinary perspective critical to the agency's programs that cannot be provided by anyone else. At one meeting, one of the representatives spoke with such candor that I found it disarming. This person's level of self-awareness and courage deepened my appreciation of the hardships this individual faces every day but continues to carry on with life. Their voices at the table underscore the importance of the work of this nonprofit that serves them.*

*Category 2:* Those who are influential in the community. With a compound growth rate of over 5 percent each year, nonprofits are sprouting up everywhere. Combine this with the rise of social cause movements, it takes more than just awareness of the organization for it to have an impact on people's perception. Community influencers have a special voice that breaks through the noise, and their advocacy at critical times is extraordinarily powerful.

*When I served as chair of the board for the school of the arts foundation I mentioned earlier, we conducted a detailed process that considered each of these criteria. As we considered this category, one of the board members offered, "the*

*parent of one of the teachers at the school has been written
up in a number of articles in the local media about her role
in making our community an arts community. She serves on
a number of boards and has received awards for her service
and leadership." Perfect. I set up an appointment and went to
visit her. I described what we were trying to accomplish, and
she was "all in." At one of our board meetings, she pulled out
a list of influential people in the community and said, "if you
write the letter, I'll sign it." And she followed up with personal
phone calls. Her ability to position us in the community was
unmatched. And her name on the letterhead gave us instant
credibility when I asked the mayor to speak at an event. It
also opened doors with other community organizations that
had not perceived our foundation as an important part of the
arts community.*

*Category 3:* Affluent philanthropists who love your cause. Not
everyone who is affluent is philanthropic, so this is an important
distinction. These individuals are indispensable, not only for
their generous financial support, but because of their loyalty to
organizations they trust, their concern for substantial program
impact, and their circles of influence. Obviously, with wealth
comes influence and sometimes undue influence. Attracting a
number of wealthy individuals to serve on your board mitigates
this risk. But, keep in mind again, that recruiting for character
and competence precedes recruiting for connections. All board
members must possess the first two.

*Early in my consulting practice, I was hired by the board
of a nonprofit to conduct an internal audit. It was actually*

*being funded by the organization's primary donor. As I got to know this individual over the next few years, we often mused about the light and dark side of his extraordinary philanthropy to this organization. It was his passion, so he contributed generously each year. His concerns, and rightfully so, were, first, that the organization was too dependent upon him and his connections, second, that his philanthropy was inhibiting the growth of the fundraising program, and third, that his philanthropy gave him undue influence on the organization—as he was aware his funding affected the course of the organization.*

*In response, the board placed a special emphasis on its recruiting outreach. While still seeking a balance in its composition, board members focused on attracting other affluent individuals—though not all as board members, but rather as true believers who were connected in one way or another. Some were recruited as committee members, others as informal advisors. The chair also pursued a strategy wherein he scaled back his funding as the organization sought to expand its network of high wealth donors. Wisely, the organization created a position for a major gifts officer laser-focused on building the pool of high wealth gift prospects.*

*It took a few years, but they did achieve a balance over time, and he was able to scale back his financial support so that it was more in keeping with the overall pool of major gift contributors.*

*Without his philanthropy, this organization would never have been able to pursue the breadth of programs in its portfolio. Without his philanthropy, it would not have had nearly the influence it has had for its cause. But, as he wisely understood, every nonprofit needs to cultivate some wealthy individuals and seek a balanced representation on its board.*

*Category 4:* Those equipped to help your organization succeed in its mission. Every nonprofit board should keep its eyes peeled for those unique people in the community who have specials skills or fill unique business niches that can offer special insight. Often, we think of lawyers, or accountants, or marketers, and yes, generally speaking, they fit the bill—and offer great value. But don't stop there. Let's say you are working in the area of affordable housing, and one day you come across this young entrepreneur who teaches mechanical engineering at the local college. He's started a business building studios and residences for local artists using shipping containers. He would definitely be someone to consider. The point is, keep in touch with your business journals and local media with an eye to the next great fit for your board.

*I saw this in action a few years ago when one of my clients, a small affordable housing nonprofit, was looking to develop new, innovative housing options. It had a tiny staff. One day the executive director was introduced to a young man who worked for a community foundation and had a passion for affordable housing. He had done his research and was extraordinarily well-informed. The CEO invited him to serve on the board, and he was not only able to identify new sources of funding, but he accessed connections in the community that could yield new, cooperative relationships for the nonprofit.*

When boards engage thoughtfully in this process, they discover that they expand their influence by engaging these individuals, and they also expand their awareness of new issues and perspectives that improve the board's effectiveness. It takes time and effort—but it is achievable. And the results are rewarding.

Once you have a clear sense of those "connecting" people you are seeking, start talking to your friends and associates. Once you start, you might be surprised at how connected you are across the community. I experienced this a few years ago when I was a guest at a board meeting where board members were asked to identify people who might be interested in the organization and its cause. My immediate response was, gee, I don't think I know anyone. But I took out my phone and reviewed the names on my contacts list. I found eight people that might have an interest in the organization who possessed the ability to connect the organization to a broader audience—and I gave these names to the executive director. I have found this to be a consistent experience over the years—we know more people and have more connections than we think we have. I've concluded that rather than six degrees of separation, it's more like one or two.

When discussing connections, the conversation has to be larger than "who do you know?" It must be a conversation about people *who are able and willing to connect the organization to an expanded circle of influence.* And you need to think about where to find them.

It is baffling to me when boards won't consider the characteristics of those they need to recruit or where to look for them. My question is: How can you find what you need if you don't know what you are looking for or where to look for it? It reminds me of the familiar story of the guy who was crawling around at the base of a lamppost one night when someone asked, "What are you looking for?" The man replied, "Something fell out of my pocket. I know it must be important, but I don't know what it is." The visitor said, "Well, at least you were lucky enough to drop it by a lamppost." "Oh, I didn't," he replied, "it fell out of my pocket down the street, but the light is better here."

Back to the foundation board:

*We set about making a list of people who need to know us and assigned board members to make initial contacts. We also set up a practice where at least two current board members interviewed every potential board member. During this process, I was insistent that we develop an interview guide and stick to the questions. And I made myself available to take part in each interview—until I felt confident that other board members would stick to the script—which, candidly, proved to be elusive.*

*I was glad that I insisted on the interview guide and my participation. Prospective board member interviews are susceptible to becoming overly casual conversations because volunteers can feel uncomfortable conducting a real interview. They benefit from more-experienced guidance to stay on course. In this case, I could model the right approach to the interview. I noticed that those interviewing with me were relieved that I took the lead role. I'm not saying this is true of everyone. Some people are terrific interviewers.*

*There was an order to our process. First, I had conversations with current board members who had not been active. I asked them whether they wanted to continue. If they did, I laid out the expectations. Though bittersweet, those not engaged resigned. Over the coming weeks, we developed a list of new people that fit each of the categories, and we started meeting with them. After several months we had a new board that included a prominent community leader who was an arts advocate, the publisher of a local newspaper, a manager at a prominent performing arts center, a well-connected musician, two teachers, and two parents.*

*By the end of the year, thanks to the connections of the board members, we attracted a nationally recognized performing artist group who performed two concerts at well below cost—one for the kids that included a dialog about being an artist and one for the community. The school's eight-hundred-seat auditorium was packed for the public performance, which also featured performances by the students. The mayor spoke about the importance of arts education at the opening, and the local news picked it up as one of the top three concerts of the year. All of this goes to the bottom line—the school was now on the map, the kids enjoyed an opportunity to talk with professional artists, they performed in front of a large audience, and we created a special fund to provide instruments to children who couldn't afford them.*

*Though I am not an advocate for raising money solely through events, our purpose was to connect to the community, to communicate our mission, and to show the impact we were having. Everyone in the theater that night was moved. The artists on stage spoke passionately about the importance of arts education for children. And at one point, everyone in the theater was standing and clapping. If you were there that night, you could not resist being influenced deeply by our mission.*

# Practical Exercise

Making connections with those who will expand your circle of influence is not an onerous task, but it takes discipline and a cadence of accountability that is championed by the chair of the board.

Start by setting aside sufficient time at a board meeting or by calling a special session. Board members and senior staff should begin the session by brainstorming all the various connections that will expand the organization's circle of influence. I like to use small groups so that everyone gets a voice and, usually, each group has a different perspective that adds to the richness of the conversation when the whole group is reconvened. Be careful not to judge anyone's ideas in the beginning. Instead, let the creative juices flow. Be open to new or even wild ideas, release assumptions, and be receptive to different points of view.

The CEO and the chief advancement officer play essential roles in that they likely know the players in the community. I recommend that they put together a list with an accompanying rationale to set the stage for a discussion. I have found that board members respond better when someone kindles the conversation with something they can respond to.

Using the categories listed in this section, discuss the profile of individuals that fit each category. (Here again, the board chair and CEO may want to take a crack at describing them before the meeting.) For example, when considering the category of "those you serve," describe them. What are the attributes of an individual from this category that can contribute to effective governance? When considering those who are influential, where do you need influence? What are you seeking to achieve through this influence?

And again, what are the characteristics of the person who will be most helpful with gaining influence where it is needed?

Write it down and distribute it to board members. Again, if you know what you are looking for, you are likely to find it. As I wrote above, I was surprised to discover all of the people I knew who would be fit for an organization when I just took a moment to think about it. Using this process also breaks down board member resistance to sharing names.

Once you finish this exercise, turn it over to a working group, task force, or committee that will take responsibility to make this an ongoing process and report progress regularly to the board. The board chair and the committee should be sure to engage the entire board throughout the year. One way to kindle this is to ask at each board meeting, "Has anyone met someone you think might be a candidate for board membership?" Another approach is to have the committee chair talk about one or more of the board member profile characteristics and ask board members if they know individuals who would make a good fit. Again, it's creating a cadence that always reminds board members to consider candidates. Though the committee is responsible for managing the process, connecting the organization to the community is everyone's job. Just because there is a committee working on it does not absolve members of their responsibilities.

Following are few core questions to use to guide a conversation with any prospective candidate. Feel free to add to the list. Though the questions may change in form from person to person, by the end of the conversation, you are likely to have a good handle on the person's connections.

• How do you imagine helping our organization in the community?

• Where do you think our organization should make connections that would help strengthen its reputation and mission delivery?

• Its programs?

• Its fundraising?

• Where do you think you could help our organization make those connections and build relationships?

• Would you be willing to take an active role in making connections, building relationships, and assisting with outreach?

# CHAPTER 5

# Composition

Composition: *how various elements of the whole are combined and relate to one another.*

When approaching this topic, it is important to remember that the fundamental purpose of a governing board is oversight. Its fiduciary responsibility is to ensure that the nonprofit is true to its mission, that its programs are aligned with it and serving the purpose for which they are intended, that the finances are well-managed, and that it complies with its bylaws, all state and federal laws, and all other applicable regulations.

Since a nonprofit does not typically pay income taxes, it falls under the auspices of the public trust. It is the obligation of the governing board to ensure its composition is representative of the public it serves. One might say, "That isn't necessary because all kind, open-minded, and generous people are competent to care for the community the organization serves, and thus competent to govern." Although this may appear reasonable, history has not borne this out. Research clearly demonstrates that we all carry biases, many of which are unconscious. To truly represent the communities we serve, we must have representatives of those communities—who carry the perspectives and concerns of those communities—on our boards.

This means that diversity, inclusion, and equity are essential concerns for nonprofits—and governing boards are the trustees. Diversity in the nonprofit world means that board membership reflects the demographics and perspectives of those it serves—as well as those who might help it serve them better. It also means that the composition of board membership represents a cross-section of people in the communities the organization serves—whether race, ethnicity, gender, age, education, profession, occupation, income level, geography, sexual preference, marital status, etc. Even beyond this obligation, more diverse boards are more effective in fulfilling their organizations' missions.

As Jennifer Hudson, President of ThinkBeyond Public Relations, said upon reviewing this chapter, "My hope is that diversity and inclusion become a mindset and a part of the natural order of things, so much that it is as unconscious and second nature as breathing. It's visionary, I know, but the organizations that embrace it in a real and authentic way will be most successful."

I have found this chapter the most difficult to write because I don't want to diminish the challenges faced by individuals whose identity has not yet been fully embraced and included with equity in our society. Of all groups, women appear to have made the greatest strides forward in last few decades in regard to these issues. But, even for women, inclusion and equity are still not on par with men. I admit up front that I do not explicitly address the challenges faced by the LGBTQ community, older adults, people with disabilities, and so many others, but in the examples I do use I note how these issues affect all those who experience discrimination and exclusion because they are not part of the majority.

I do give greater attention to the Black community, which comprises individuals who have faced a long, difficult struggle to achieve inclusion and equity. This is not meant to imply that others have not. But I made this choice in this moment in history when racial justice may have reached an inflection point, an opportunity for transformation. I hope to do my part to nudge it forward.

Boards should be concerned about diversity, inclusion, and equity, not only because it is a fiduciary responsibility, but because it is important to the future of our society and the aspirations of our children. As one CEO told me recently: "Look at the clients we serve and look at the frontline staff—they are a very diverse population. When these people see a culturally diverse board, it has a tremendous impact on their sense of hope and wellbeing. Their beliefs about the possibilities are transformed when they see people like themselves in the composition of the board—and the senior management team. This was driven home for me on the day Barrack Obama was elected President. My son walked into the kitchen and said, 'I could be president someday.' Seeing a black president deeply influenced my son's perception of what is now possible."

In contrast to diversity, inclusion is about the mindset and behaviors of board members, not the attributes of the candidate. Inclusion means that members of the board create an environment that fosters a true sense of belonging for everyone; that steps are taken to ensure that each board member is empowered to participate; and that everyone is treated fairly and respectfully. In sum, everyone is offered an authentic opportunity to contribute without bias or exclusion to the organization's governance responsibilities.

Equity is defined as being just, impartial and fair. In the boardroom setting it means providing board members, individually, with the resources and support they need to fully participate. I emphasize "individually" because people are different. Each individual has unique needs that must be addressed in order to participate to her fullest potential. In order to ensure and sustain equity, the board must acknowledge this and fully commit to addressing it in policy and practice.

In years past, we often used the term equality. The intent was to promote fairness and justice by ensuring that everyone gets the same things. The problem with this concept is that equality is only fair and just if everyone is starting at the same place with the same needs. This is simply not true.

For governing boards, equity means taking a careful look at your nonprofit's circumstances, policies, practices, and attitudes to amend those not aligned with the principles of equity. Meet people where they are and provide resources and support tailored to their needs.

## Diversity and Inclusion

As we scan the landscape of nonprofit boards, we find that many are neither diverse nor inclusive. Though there continues to be an improvement, a recent BoardSource survey revealed that many do not see this as an issue.

The 2017 report by BoardSource revealed what some describe as disturbing attitudes among board members regarding diverse and inclusive board composition. The report titled "Leading with Intent: BoardSource Index of Nonprofit Board Practices" found that "Boards are no more diverse than they were two years ago, and current recruitment priorities indicate this is unlikely to change." The report explains, "Despite reporting high levels of dissatisfaction with current board demographics—particularly racial and ethnic diversity—boards are not prioritizing demographics in their recruitment practices. Nearly a fifth of all chief executives report they are not prioritizing demographics in their board recruitment strategy, despite being dissatisfied with their board's racial and ethnic diversity."

At the 2018 Association for Research on Nonprofit Organizations and Voluntary Action Conference, Professor Chris Fredette of the University of Windsor pointed out that even Google failed to significantly increase diversity and inclusion after investing millions of dollars to achieve it.

In its 2019 report, "The Governance Gap: Examining Diversity and Equity on Nonprofit Boards of Directors," the firm Koya Leadership Partners states: "...we've seen how difficult it is for boards and organizations that aren't diverse or inclusive to recruit and retain leaders of color. Boards that are overwhelmingly homogeneous are often not even aware of how their composition affects their ability to effectively attract or assess candidates with different backgrounds and experiences."

While seventy percent of the boards surveyed said they were not content with the current level of diversity and inclusion, seventy-four percent do not have a written statement or policy for diversity and inclusion. Only nineteen percent provide training on diversity and inclusion. About forty percent of boards described as having medium to low diversity have not implemented recruiting efforts designed to attract members of diverse backgrounds. And when asked why, fifty-one percent said it was because of lack of access to qualified candidates, twenty-one percent said it was geography, and eighteen percent said it was due to lack of resources.

These findings are quite striking. What is going on here? In the following pages I hope to shed light on the true obstacles, which I am convinced are not access to candidates, geography, or lack of resources.

As I am writing this in 2020, conversations around racial and social justice are in full force. They highlight core underlying issues at play that affect our ability to achieve diversity, inclusion and equity throughout our culture. Hopefully, this conversation will create a different future where visual cues, such as skin color or physique, are not associated with the negative presumptions that have historically disenfranchised entire groups.

What are these underlying factors? Though I am sure there are many, let me highlight the ones that stand out to me.

## Social Categorization

Our brain uses categories to help us efficiently process information. Research suggests this process is active in infancy; and that it is spontaneous, occurring without much thought. We even enjoy placing ourselves in categories as we move through life to promote an identity. Just look at the popularity of college hoodies, or sports team jerseys, or the neighborhoods we aspire to live in, or the cars we buy, or the brands we prefer.

Though we find categorization helpful, it is fraught with errant assumptions and bias when we apply it to others—and we often do it unconsciously. As you recruit board members, even as you identify and name various demographic types, you risk introducing the bias of social categories. When we place individuals in a 'type' category, there is a tendency for us to lose sight of them as individuals. Instead, we respond to them as a social construct—older, gay, poor, etc.

When we see people as representing a particular category, we mentally emphasize the characteristics that fit that category in our minds while we pay little to no attention to their individual differences or unique characteristics. We make immediate inferences and assumptions about individuals when we don't even know them.

During recruitment, it is extraordinarily important for board members to be conscious of such biases and focus on seeing people, whom they seek to recruit to diversify membership, as unique individuals who bring important—often unheard or underrepresented—perspectives because of their experiences in life.

## Implicit Bias

*One thing that I have to deal with as a Black man, who is often the only Black person or one of less than five, on a board or in an executive environment is the exhausting exercise of navigating the current of norms and behaviors of the group. Even when boards do recruit a "diverse" candidate who looks differently and thinks differently than the group it is exhausting for that individual to speak from another mindset.*

*This is my reality.*

*I have been called "angry" (yes, the dreaded "angry black man") because after multiple failed attempts to use data and professional literature to make the case for equity, I have used a sterner tone with the group to reiterate the data. Keep in mind my tone is never any sterner than that of another member of the board who would happen to be from the majority culture of the board. There is a double-standard if you will (one viewed to be "passionate" or just a little "aggressive" while the other is called "angry"). Majority-culture boards tend to isolate the new thoughts of the diverse board member and label it as angry, which is why so many people from diverse backgrounds may choose not to serve on these boards. It can be an energy vampire for sure.*

This poignant narrative from a highly accomplished executive cuts through the fog to the heart of the issue. And this issue is not only encountered by Black men. Women, minorities, people with disabilities, members of the LGBTQ community, and even older adults constantly encounter cultures rife with implicit bias.

Implicit bias is one of the greatest barriers to diversity, inclusion, and equity. Implicit bias describes the situation in which people speak and act based on prejudice and stereotypes without intending to do so. How this occurs is the subject of loads of research on how the mind functions.

From our earliest years, we learn how to make sense of the world, how to be safe, and how to satisfy our needs through our physical experiences and through what others teach us. As we age, we develop higher reasoning through our neocortex. This is the location of intelligence, intuition, imagination, and understanding. It's the location of our higher cognitive abilities where we develop philosophies and belief systems that guide our rational thinking. Nevertheless, we still carry with us our amygdala, often called our fight-or-flight center. Here reside unconscious triggers that are activated by life circumstances. And sometimes, these triggers result in actions inconsistent with our stated beliefs. Implicit bias is not just triggered by unconscious reaction, it is also the symptom of enculturation, wherein we gradually take on the characteristics and norms of the majority group. Within these norms are embedded latent biases. I will address this further in the next section.

Some implicit biases become embarrassingly self-evident; like when we recognize as we get to know people that we have misjudged them based on appearance or first impression. But often, it is more complex.

For example, Jack (fictitious name) sees himself as a feminist and believes in the equality of women. He is a vocal advocate. Yet, when he goes somewhere with a woman colleague, he insists on driving. He races ahead to open the door, whether or not he has been given any cues to do so. And when one looks carefully at his management practices, he has promoted more men than women, and on average, women on his team are not equally compensated.

Pam (fictitious name) is a young, mid-level manager at a retail electronics company. She speaks with pride about hiring people with disabilities and older adults with mobility limitations. She often brags about her company's diversity policy and is quick to show the statistics. Yet, her sales strategy meetings are mostly filled with Millennials. When pressed for a reason, she says the people with disabilities and older adults have enough challenges just dealing with everyday life. These meetings are high stress, and I don't want to tax them.

Implicit bias is difficult to see in ourselves. It takes courage and receptivity to listen to others when they call out evidence of it in our lives. But to move forward into a diverse, inclusive, and equitable environment, we all must take a close look at our behaviors and make a change when what we do isn't consistent with what we say; or when we recognize it is hurtful and unfair.

Harvard offers a wonderful online tool to check biases. It is called *Project Implicit* and can be found at https://implicit.harvard. edu/implicit/takeatest.html. You can log on and take several exercises to gauge whether you are holding unconscious biases that are affecting your judgment. There are exercises to test your implicit bias in regard to all sorts of categories: Native American, Transgender, Asian, people with disabilities, older Americans, and more. In these times, wherein we struggle to achieve diversity, inclusion, and equity, I recommend these exercises for every board member.

What do you do once you've taken an exercise? It's not about determining whether you are biased, it's about unplugging for a moment to be mindful and reflective, to dig a little deeper into the way you think.

I would like to suggest that you take at least one of the Harvard exercises. Assume the answers are a true reflection—even if you feel a bit of resistance. Then ask yourself, what might have influenced my way of thinking? Where might I have blind spots? What might I do differently or better? Self-assessment is challenging and, maybe even a bit painful, but when we engage in it honestly, we become better people.

But don't stop with personal reflection. Make this a topic for deep, engaged discussion within the boardroom. Bringing these issues into the daylight of open, honest, and receptive conversation offers the greatest promise for change. Reach out to professionals who can help you carry the conversation further. There are a number of professionals well-versed in this issue who can guide such a discussion. If you cannot afford this, there are numerous excellent, free webinars available on the Internet. I believe it will make you a better board member and build a stronger board.

## Enculturation

Enculturation is the process by which a person learns, accepts, and adjusts to the norms of a group—which are usually congruent with the opinions and perspectives of the majority or the powerful within that group. Minorities enculturate so that they can function within the larger cultural framework or society where they live, work, and socialize.

In regard to the manner in which enculturation impacts our nonprofits, it was powerfully brought home to me when an executive told me the story of one of his first days on the job. His assistant, a woman, walked into his office with a cup of coffee. He asked her, "Why do you feel you need to bring me coffee? I can make my own." I'm sure it caught her by surprise, but I bet she appreciated it.

In another funny, but painfully true story, a newly appointed executive recounted what occurred when he first met a colleague. She just stared at him. When he asked what was wrong, she said, "You're the unicorn!" "What?" he asked. She said, "You are a black man who is the CEO of a nonprofit. That is very rare." He went on to share a number of incidents where clients and front-line staffers were surprised that he wasn't White or a woman... He explained how he had to help them understand his leadership role and style because they were not used to working for an organization where the CEO was Black. He described how they knew how to act around a White CEO or a woman, they had years of enculturation, but it took time for them to learn how to relate to him.

As I explored the implications of enculturation with executives, one offered, "too often we fall prey to the maxim 'If it ain't broke, don't fix it.' But maybe our expectations are just too low." I thought of a simple example to clarify the concept. Let's say it takes two hours for your dryer to dry a load of clothes. At first look, it's running just fine. The power is on, the clothes are tumbling, and it's hot. Living under the maxim that 'if it ain't broke don't fix it,' you just accept that the dryer just performs this way. But what if you broke free from that habit of thinking and asked, "I wonder if it could be changed? Improved?" So, you take a deeper look into how the dryer is operating and you discover that the vent has become choked with lint. So, you clean out the vent, and now the dryer is operating with very high efficiency, drying clothes in half the time. You freed yourself from a habit of thought that had kept you stuck in errant assumptions.

As board members, we all need to take a hard look at the board's habits of thinking. Are we or other members stuck in a habit of thinking that assumes 'this is just the way things work?' The evolving demographic profile of our country continues to change. In just a few decades, some majorities will be minorities. If our nonprofit boards don't question the dominant cultural mores that dictate habits of thought, the sector is destined to lose ground in recruiting effective board members that reflect the demographics of our society, and especially the beliefs and values of the vast diversity of perspectives important to building healthy communities.

In an email exchange with a Black executive about enculturation, he illuminated a dimension that merits attention. He wrote:

*I heard this phrase and it may help explain what I mean, "when you speak with one Black person you have spoken with one Black person"... meaning, the shared attribute of extra melanin in the skin does not mean one Black person can speak for the whole or that the thoughts of that Black person are different than the already enculturated norms of the group. This is important if the majority White board members say, "we are recruiting for 'diversity'" and the Black person they identify has the same socio-economic, political, and religious background. This means there is just one more person who thinks like the enculturated majority but just looks different.*

Though spoken from the perspective of a Black man, this is relevant to individuals who represent the various categories of diversity.

Finally, enculturation is hard to see through a process of self-reflection alone because it is so deeply rooted in our assumptions and presuppositions. It takes an independent observer to help us see our biases, deficiencies, and unproductive habits. To that end, I recommend regularly tapping into the talent of a diversity expert or, as one executive described to me, "an anti-enculturation champion," to shine a bright light on the culture. This way you have an opportunity to see whether you all see things the same way, and what needs to be done about it.

## Distrust

Those who have not been included reasonably question the motives of those whom have always been included. When reaching out to these individuals, experiencing their distrust, overtly or covertly, should not be surprising. They might be wondering when you approach them, "Are you trying to look good to your constituency?" "Do you need something from me to further your own interests?" "Are you striving to look politically correct?" Or if someone has had an experience like my colleague I wrote about in the last section, they may reasonably conclude: "Why are you asking me when I know I won't be heard?"

As a White man, when I served as executive director of a program focused on helping people in depressed communities, I often experienced skepticism. I was once asked by a local official, "What is a White man doing working in this neighborhood?" It was a fair question. What were my motives? To advance my career? To feel good about me? Or to use my skills and talent to work within the community with existing neighborhood organizations to bring about productive change. I always thought and hoped it was the latter. With the guidance of a community development specialist, we created a consortium of local organizations that focused on different aspects of the communities' needs. Because I understood that my life experience was not at all similar to those we served, I hired managers and social workers who grew up or lived in these communities or ones that were similar. Over the next year we were able to put together a functioning consortium of service providers to jointly seek funding and to collaborate across our organizations to serve those in need.

If you are one of the board members assigned to outreach, it is important to be receptive to others doubting your motives. Don't take it personally. Honor it and respond honestly. In preparation, it's worthwhile to do your own personal motives-check. What might be your implicit biases? Are you clear on why you want this person on the board? Are you committed to diversity, inclusiveness, and equity because you believe in it? It is important to really work on self-awareness before the conversation. Taking time to examine your beliefs and motives enables you to be more spontaneous and receptive during the conversation.

In addition to self-awareness, I have found that transparency is a powerful approach to dealing with distrust. Sometimes distrust is hard to identify. It may be that candidates never return your calls. Or, without discussion, they immediately and politely refuse. Or they might tell you right to your face, it's not me you are looking for. My advice is to be honest and upfront from the first words out of your mouth. Describe how you came to be assigned this job. Talk about the board discussions that brought you to this point. Explain why the board has decided on this course of action. Be clear about why you are reaching out specifically to these individuals. Explain what the board is seeking and the unique qualifications that each individual brings to the board. Further describe what the board expects each person to contribute. Remember, people may not feel comfortable serving on the board as minorities. If you sense this is part of the resistance, make sure you show that you understand this as a valid concern—and discuss how it can be addressed.

# Tokenism

There is another common pitfall in board governance practices that causes a different set of problems through misguided good intentions. This is the organization that completes a detailed chart that lists all the "diverse" attributes it seeks in forming its board. These attributes usually include business or professional acumen, such as marketing, human resources, law, finance, and maybe demographic categories, such as age, gender and identity, race, ethnicity, and geographic location. Here is what it might look like:

| | | Candidate | | | | | | |
|---|---|---|---|---|---|---|---|---|
| | | 1 | 2 | 3 | 4 | 5 | 6 | 7 |
| **Attributes** | Lawyer | X | | X | | | X | |
| | Marketer | | X | | | | | X |
| | Finance | | | | X | X | | |
| | Millennial | | | | X | | | X |
| | Diverse | X | X | | | X | X | |
| | Wealthy | X | X | | | X | X | |

I once worked with a board that satisfied all of these types of criteria, but it continued to flounder because members were not competent in governance. They continually became immersed in operations, lending their professional expertise, and directing the management team—which couldn't thrive because board members who only knew operations, not governance, micromanaged the team.

In their attempts to strengthen diversity and inclusion, boards like this act out of good intentions, but they fail to consider governance ability and thus suffered the consequences.

When viewed from the outside, these boards may appear enlightened, but they start at the wrong place. They are "diversifying" by recruiting members based on business acumen and personal attributes—ethnicity, gender, age, socio-economic status, etc. They are seeking some candidates just because they fit a diversity category—and in all of my years I've never seen a category titled diversity of thought.

Plain and simple, this is tokenism.

Recruiting members as tokens of a diversity category is one of the worst things a board can do in its recruitment process. It is the result of *not* seeking candidates for their competence, character, connections, and the perspective they bring—as I discuss in earlier chapters. But rather, it is satisfying a quota or creating an optic that looks good on grant proposals.

It is concerning that even with the cultural imperative toward board diversity, many boards don't view it as a priority. If boards do not grasp the fundamental cultural and organizational value of diversity, they are prone to fall prey to tokenism because it appears like an easy fix or, in some cases, an uninformed rush to do the right thing. Let me give you an example.

*The chair of the board of a national organization came to me because he was disappointed with the performance of the board. He expressed concern that the interests of the organization's constituency weren't fully represented. There were members of the board that represented those served by the organization, but it wasn't turning out to be the diverse and inclusive representation as they had intended.*

*Why?*

*In this instance, the board had gotten itself in a particularly uncomfortable position. An individual selected to represent a marginalized constituency served by the organization was impeding progress. He was acting out a self-serving personal agenda. He would disrupt board meetings with tangential issues, make politically incorrect statements in public, and push the organization to attend to his personal interests. He could not see the larger picture and was unable to hold true to the interests and concerns of those he was chosen to represent.*

*Since this individual was an elected member of the board representing a minority perspective, there was nothing he or the board could do to gracefully part ways. Instead, they spent his term minimizing the damage—which required a lot of staff time as well.*

*Upon reflection, the board chair understood that the best of intentions to include representation from a marginalized group had failed. Without the proper vetting of this individual's competence and character they had achieved only a token of representation, not the real thing.*

*The good news is they learned their lesson very well. They continued to recruit board members who represented their marginalized constituencies but vetted them very carefully. In the ensuing years, they gained greater trust from this community and were able to powerfully advocate for the issues of their cause through the voices of those most impacted.*

## Ignorance and Want

I can hear some of you saying, "What?!? These are pretty archaic terms to be used in a business book." Bear with me for a moment. The gap between those that have and those that do not continues to grow. And this is most evident in the communities of people who are not represented on most of our nonprofit governing boards.

When I work with clients, I present the trends in income and giving. In the thirty-five years between 1980 and 2014, the average annual growth in income for middle-class Americans decreased from 2 percent per annum to 1 percent per annum. The income growth of those in the lowest 5 percent dropped to below zero—i.e., they make less each year. The top 1 percent of income earners grew by 2.5 percent per annum, and the top .001 percent grew by 5 percent per annum. As of 2012, the top 10 percent of income earners were earning 52 percent of all earned income in the United States. These are striking and undeniable trends in the distribution of wealth in our country. (Source: Thomas Piketty, Emmanuel Saez, and Gabriel Zucman; Jessia Ma and Stuart A. Thompson. This data is consistent with more recent studies that are underway. I recommend The United States Congress Joint Economic Committee report, "Measuring Income Concentration—A Guide for the Confused.")

In the closing pages of *A Christmas Carol*, Charles Dickens pens in the voice of the Ghost of Christmas Present, "They are Man's and they cling to me, appealing from their fathers. This boy is *Ignorance*. This girl is *Want*. Beware them both, and all of their degree; but most of all beware this boy, for on his brow I see that written which is Doom, unless the writing be erased."

Though it might be an obscure reference for some, I feel the Dicken's quote is central to our conversation about the importance of diversity, inclusion, and equity among our governing boards. Want is increasing. If nonprofit boards truly are responsible for the public trust, they need to ensure that they are truly trustees in regard to this social issue and their organization's mission.

What about ignorance? Though Dickens was likely commenting on the lack of education that keeps people from improving their socio-economic status, I am emphasizing the "ignore" aspect of ignorance. If we trace the word's etymology, it means "lacking wisdom or knowledge, unaware, to be unacquainted, to mistake or misunderstand." And most importantly, "to take no notice of or pay no attention to."

Although some have told me they see signs of improvement, according to the evidence presented earlier in this chapter, nonprofit governing boards that are overwhelmingly homogeneous are often not aware of how their composition affects their ability to effectively attract or assess candidates with different backgrounds and experiences. Despite reporting high levels of dissatisfaction with current board demographics—particularly racial and ethnic diversity—boards are not prioritizing demographics in their recruitment practices.

This is not just the plight of the nonprofit sector. It has failed to be addressed in the corporate sector for decades. The Governor of California has signed a law that requires boards of public companies located in California to include directors from "underrepresented communities." Such legislation fails to address the underlying challenges that must be addressed to achieve authentic change. Such a law will achieve the appearance of diversity while failing to achieve it—because it does not address issues like enculturation.

However one defines it, the lack of diversity, inclusion, and equity is an expression of ignorance. And as Dickens warns, if we fail to take appropriate notice and if we fail to become acquainted with the implications of our inaction, and thus do nothing about diversity and inclusion, we fail in our core responsibility to be caretakers of the public trust.

We need not remain in ignorance. We have an opportunity to act differently and change the course of the future. If governing boards are going to play their appointed role, board members must take note and take action to create diverse, inclusive, and equitable boards. We can achieve this if we have the awareness and willpower to start doing things differently.

## Crossing the Threshold into the World of Diverse and Inclusive Boards

Where does a board begin this process of transformation? Start with the premise that all candidates must satisfy the capacity-to-serve criteria laid out in the recruitment profile.

The responsibility of the board is, then, to immerse itself in an authentic process that pursues diversity, inclusion, and equity.

Someone has asked me, "Isn't this reverse discrimination?" For all of the reasons I have outlined in this chapter, clearly it is not reverse discrimination. It is changing practices of exclusion and enculturation that stifle inclusion and diversity, fostering an "us versus them" mentality. It is only us.

I'm not writing about only race and ethnicity. There is gender, sexual identity and preference, socio-economic status, location, age, religion… an expansive number of demographic criteria that describe those who have not been included or treated fairly and equitably.

Building a competent, inclusive board takes commitment and work. Yet the near- and longer-term consequences of not doing so can weigh heavily upon the organization's effectiveness and reputation—from lost opportunity due to lack of diverse viewpoints, to failure to serve the community because it is not represented, to brand damage because groups feel disenfranchised or patronized.

Beyond recruitment activities, provide leadership by creating cultures and environments that embrace diversity and inclusion. When I ask boards to consider "those you serve" and "those equipped to help the organization better succeed at its mission," I emphasize diversity and inclusion. We must recruit all board members for the contribution they can make to the cause—and through paying attention to diversity, we further enrich our culture.

How do we avoid these pitfalls and recruit a competent and appropriately diverse board?

Start with a thoughtful board interview process. By doing so, you gain insight into how individuals process information and make decisions, how skilled they are at governance, and the unique perspectives that they can offer. By employing a thoughtful interview process, you can create a balanced portfolio of candidates.

Building a strong board that embodies the character, competence, connections, and diversity of thought that organizations need to thrive is not a complicated process. Actually, the approach is straightforward, but it takes time and discipline to do it right. And in a world in which attention spans appear to be diminishing, this requires boards to make this an intentional, explicit process.

There is probably a book that could be written on the importance of the proper mindset in governance. Thoughtfulness, preparation, and planning are tremendously important. As Abraham Lincoln said, "Give me six hours to chop down a tree, and I will spend the first four sharpening the ax."

Thoughtfulness must include careful self-reflection.

# Practical Exercise

Engage the full board and senior staff in a discussion of the organization's values, the attributes of the diverse culture it wants to establish in the organization, and its responsibility to own and embody them.

Following this discussion, identify the additional culture and character attributes, competencies, and community connections needed for the board to thrive. Everyone must be on the same page. This chart provides a simple but effective template.

| Board Member Recruitment Attributes | | | | |
|---|---|---|---|---|
| | Culture Attributes | Character Attributes | Competencies | Community Connections |
| All Candidates Must Have | | | | |
| Some Candidates Must Have | | | | |
| Note: This is a basic framework. You may identify characteristics that fall outside of these four basic categories. If they help identify the right candidates, by all means, include them. | | | | |

When you build your board profile, use both categories under each "C": one that lists the characteristics that "all must have" and one that lists those that "some must have." The top row is non-negotiable, while the second captures attributes that not all candidates possess (but some must).

Once the board has completed the assessment, create a written recruitment profile. This profile is your guide to identifying viable candidates and suspects within board members' circles of influence. Use it to consider the various venues where viable candidates are found. As one colleague offered, "small, deliberate acts" can work powerfully to bring about change. So, step outside your comfort zone and get to know people who you don't usually engage—and talk with them about your intentions. Don't hesitate to share the characteristics you are seeking throughout board members' networks. There may be associations, agencies, or consultants in your community that specialize in leadership development and diversity. An informed, competent advisor can add great value to the process.

This is the perfect time to integrate *Project Implicit* into your recruitment process and to have a thoughtful discussion of the findings. To encourage open discussion, you might benefit from a process in which you keep the results anonymous, but identify the number of board members whose results revealed implicit bias. Confidentiality lowers the barrier to achieving a candid discussion.

If you find a number of candidates, try using a technique called "partition dependence." In a paper titled "Let's choose one of each: Using the partition dependence effect to increase diversity in organizations," published in the journal *Organizational Behavior and Human Decision Processes*, Volume 158, May 2020, pages 11-26, an international group of four scholars (Zhiyu Feng, Yukun Liu, Zhen

Wang, and Krishna Savani) presented their findings on an approach that has proven to increase diversity in recruitment.

The process is surprisingly simple. As the authors instruct, "put all resumes of candidates from well-represented backgrounds in subfolders, but put resumes of candidates from under-represented backgrounds in the main folder (without grouping them into subfolders). The folders can be named 'Batch 1,' 'Batch 2,' etc. to avoid explicitly drawing attention to the grouping."

The authors continue, "Importantly, this intervention does not restrict (those responsible for recruitment) in any way—they are absolutely free to choose whichever candidates that they want. It only draws attention to qualified minority candidates...."

They offer one caveat:

*One limitation of our nudging strategy is that if [people] have strong biases against a particular group, then putting candidates from that group into a separate category has no effect on their [recruitment] decisions—they're still unlikely to select someone from that group. This nudge is only likely to work when [those responsible for recruitment] don't have strong biases against a particular group.*

Implement the interview process using an interview guide to engage candidates in a substantive discussion and to determine whether they are the best match. In earlier chapters of this book, I suggested a list of questions to explore candidates' competence, character, and connections. It may be useful to review them. At the end of this section I have included a core set of questions that are useful in the initial vetting of candidates.

I recommend interviewing candidates as a team, whether a combination of board members or a board member and the

CEO. This approach sends a clear message that this interview is important and that you value the candidate's time.

There is also great value in developing an interview format. This shows that you are well organized and prepared—again, an important message to send to board candidates. Some board members have well-polished skills, while others are quite new at it. If you use the guide, it will ensure a consistent series of interviews that elicit the most important information.

It is best to begin interviews with casual conversation, paying attention to the candidates, asking them to tell you a bit about themselves, what they enjoy about volunteering, and what appeals to them about this opportunity to serve in a governance capacity. As you reach out to those who have traditionally not been included, you are likely to encounter questions of your motives. In this case, I recommend re-reading the section above on distrust.

Next, it is important to talk with candidates about the values that anchor the organization and its vision—and why the nonprofit is important to the community. Share a little about the organization's value proposition and mission and give examples of programs that are serving your constituents. This is a perfect opportunity to involve the CEO in the recruitment process.

It is crucial to draw upon the candidate recruitment profile and describe what the board is seeking in candidates and why it is important. Talk about the expectations of board members as specifically as possible. It is important to lay this out to candidates before asking specific questions so that they have a sense of the landscape and whether they feel this opportunity is a match to their aspirations.

After this introduction, transition into the interview, first asking if the candidates have any questions about the organization and its programs. Then ask directly:

- Tell us a bit about your nonprofit board experience.
- How do you describe the responsibilities of governance?
- In your experience with governance, what are some practices or approaches that you think really make a difference?
- Why do you feel this opportunity is a good fit for you?
- What do you expect from fellow board members?
- Have you had any experience with fundraising?
- If you were to join the board, what do you hope to contribute?
- How do you feel about helping the organization deepen its connections to the community through your network?
- For you to feel confident that this is the right match for you, what do you need from us? From the organization itself?

I recommend that at the close of the interview you share with candidates the next steps, provide information on how candidates can contact those who interviewed them, and encourage candidates to follow up with questions. Within twenty-four hours of the interview, be sure to send a personal thank-you note that includes a few snippets regarding what you understand the candidate will contribute, based upon the conversation. Avoid a generic response. It is important to show that you listened. This sets the right tone.

With the conclusion of this chapter we have addressed the five principles related to recruitment: culture, character, competence, connections, and composition. As you implement these principles, be sure to celebrate every time you find and recruit the right people! It builds comradery among board members. It recognizes the process and reinforces in the minds of board members that it works. And it renews commitment and good feelings about the future of the organization.

# Part Two

## ONBOARDING

# CHAPTER 6

# Continuity—Part 1: Premise

**C**ontinuity: *the unbroken and consistent operation of something over a period of time.*

I grew up on a dairy farm in Upstate New York and learned a lot about electricity at a young age. Particularly how not to burn down the barn. With electrical components everywhere surrounded by dry fodder of hay, straw, and grains, proper care of electrical circuits was high on the list of responsibilities.

Electricity is an excellent metaphor for understanding continuity. Electricity is the energy of the system. It is the strength (amperage) of the electrical current and its force (voltage) that makes things work. Electrical continuity is the unimpeded flow of electrical current across circuits to achieve its purpose—through switches, conductors, electrical components, etc. Of course, for a component to function, it has to be plugged in.

When continuity is interrupted, it indicates that the electrical current is impeded or misdirected. This situation usually results in ruined components or even an electrical fire.

A well-informed homeowner understands how electricity is functioning in her home. She likely has all of the circuits mapped out at the breaker box. She knows how many circuits run through her house, the amperage of each, and what they power. If there is a problem, she can trace it to a particular circuit. That knowledge about how everything is put together is not only critical in problem-solving but essential to developing intelligence about how her house's electricity functions. She can monitor issues and, over time, see trends, strengths, and weaknesses in the system. She also knows the capacity of each circuit and whether she can add components. Or if she discovers a circuit is overloaded, she can rewire it, adding an additional circuit at its source. And if there is an emergency, she knows right where to go, which breaker to flip (or fuse to pull) to deal with the issue.

Knowledge of how a system is designed and functions and how it has performed over time is critical to ensuring continuity.

In a nonprofit organization, people are the electricity. They provide the strength (competence and commitment) and the force (authority and action) to make an organization function. They are delegated across many circuits, such as program management, fundraising, administration, governance. Members of the governing board have a special responsibility to make sure the organization is properly wired and functioning. They are the caretakers of continuity.

This is said not to diminish the role of the CEO, who might be considered the chief electrician, and an expert at that. The CEO is responsible for figuring out how to wire the organization and making sure it gets done—this is the responsibility of management. The fiduciary responsibility of the board is oversight. They are responsible for understanding how the organization has been wired and how it affects achievement of the mission. When new members are brought onto the board, it is a special obligation of the board to ensure that all members have full knowledge of how the organization is wired and how it has performed over time.

This fiduciary responsibility of the board is akin to the homeowner. Board members must know how staff are deployed and what they do, how things work, and what policies guide them. And the board, with the counsel of the CEO, should know the capacity of each circuit of the organization, where they can add and where adjustments must be made.

If there is a problem that affects organizational performance or reputation, board members must understand how everything is interconnected and be knowledgeable enough to trace the problem to its source. They must monitor issues over time to see trends, strengths, and weaknesses in the organization. And if there is an emergency, board members need to know right where to go to fix it. I am not suggesting that board members overstep into management and operations. I discuss that clear line and how it must be respected in an upcoming chapter. What I am saying is that board members must be fully informed about how the organization fits together, how it works, how energy flows through it… it's continuity.

This is not a small task and usually takes up to a year to bring a board member fully up to speed. The next two chapters will provide a detailed review of the areas of education required to help board members feel fully competent and informed.

Being fully informed is the first step. Achieving continuity requires diligence. Here is an example of what happens when continuity is broken.

*In a meeting with the chair of a board (a high-tech company executive) and the vice-chair (senior consultant with an international business management firm), we were asked to present our organizational review findings. We had just completed an in-depth study of the organization's performance and capacity. This included interviews with staff and board members, donors, accrediting agency staff members, and managers within government entities who had contracts with the organization. We had mapped out the organization's circuits, read loads of documents, reviewed the history, assessed competency, and made our recommendations.*

*Five minutes into the meeting, the chair said, "We're not going to do that..."*

The findings were straightforward—but they weren't what the chair wanted to hear.

*He wanted a simple, efficient solution—and we were pretty sure it was "fire the CEO and get a good one." However, through our in-depth interviews with all the interested parties, we learned that the highly seasoned CEO was doing a credible job in an environment where government funding was being retracted, and unreasonable expectations were being foisted on the organization.*

*Compounding the problem was a disengaged board that preferred to offer advice from the sidelines, rather than take responsibility to understand the issues, own the problems, and govern the organization. The chair and vice-chair acted as a board within a board, making decisions in isolation that affected the entire organization.*

Why is this an issue of continuity?

The chair and vice-chair lacked organizational perspective and knowledge—they did not understand the complex organizational context. They were not in touch with the organization's history and program strategy, and what is required to fulfill the mission in the current political environment. So, they didn't understand the true nature of the challenges confronting the organization, and they had lost trust in the CEO—even though he was competent.

The array of issues facing this agency formed a complex landscape that requires an engaged board willing to learn about the complexities and build trust with the CEO and his team. The human services government contract issues that brought the situation to a crisis level had happened suddenly. But warning signals along the way were missed, culminating in this crisis point. And when it became a crisis, the board and the chair were not prepared to address it. They were unable to trace the circuit to the problem because they did not understand how it was wired. Was it a failure of leadership? Of course. But whose?

*The chair became the chair because no one else wanted the job. He was familiar with his high-tech world, working in a company where he could call upon a number of staff members to solve technical problems while he focused on vision and larger issues. By contrast, he had landed at the governance helm of an organization with a lean staff and complex problems that he didn't understand. He had little experience with developing board member competence or engaging effective governance practices. His lack of connection to the executive management team and disinterest in understanding their issues made him ill-equipped to lead the governing body of the organization through this rough transition period.*

*Though in our report we had traced out the circuits and outlined the issues and solutions in detail, the chair was dismissive. Since he had not developed a trusting rapport with the executive team, he was unwilling to shepherd the process. And leading up to this situation, the board had boxed out the CEO, whom they blamed for the crisis.*

*Sadly, that was the last conversation our team had with the chair before the board fired the CEO and the CDO. Months later, when I encountered one of the board members in another setting, she confessed, "That board is a mess." Not surprisingly, she had never seen a copy of our report.*

Because of the lack of continuity—that is, because members of the board were not fully knowledgeable about how all things work and fit together, this board was stifled, overwhelmed by the complexity of the circumstances facing the organization. And that is where the chair found himself. Too many pressures and responsibilities within his business world, and this extra complexity sans the knowledge and perspective to address it left him and his fellow board members with a very unpleasant feeling: fear.

The Mayo Clinic diagnoses fear as *the unpleasant feeling triggered by the perception of danger, real or imagined.* It is not socially acceptable to admit you are afraid. But, when not called out and left to fester, fear can make us do imprudent things, as occurred in the example I just discussed.

Making rash judgments out of fear is not uncommon. Over the years, I have seen fears that have resulted in less-than-well-informed decisions. There is a long list of fears I have encountered: fear of fundraising is at the top, but also fear of planning, fear of change and innovation… an almost endless range of fears and discomforts that provoke poor choices.

You can't confront a fear by calling it out. Such an approach often makes people feel vulnerable or weak. It is important to identify its trigger. In our case, that unpleasant feeling was triggered because they were at a crisis point with insufficient knowledge or perspective to know what to do. The continuity was broken… actually, it had never been established.

In our approach, we had traced out the issues and recommended ways to rewire the organization to address the problems. With sufficient knowledge, you can break down a problem into component parts and help others see how they can manage the various pieces. It might take a bit of research to identify all of the components. But once they are identified and separated into digestible bits, you can work through them one at a time. The process builds confidence and momentum. Soon, what appeared as "too much to handle" is being managed and resolved.

Knowledge is fundamental to sustaining continuity on a governing board. In the example above, the chair's lack of historical and programmatic knowledge resulted in poor decision-making because that lack of continuity made the issue feel way too complex.

How do you ensure continuity? It requires an ongoing, intentional process of education, engagement, and trust-building.

It requires vigilance and discipline focused on board member education—especially when a new chair takes the helm. Though ensuring continuity is the board's responsibility, it must be facilitated by the CEO.

Where do you start? Create a board education program.

Some organizations produce board manuals, which can be useful. But the manual alone yields sketchy results. What works best is board engagement sessions wherein you combine storytelling with education and discovery.

Begin by outlining the topics that need to be covered. I find it most effective to organize these by subject: introduction to the organization, governance responsibilities, staff roles and responsibilities, finances, and fundraising.

It is critically important not to force-feed the board. If you cram all of the information into one session, you will defeat your purpose. Most of what you share will be forgotten. Board members must understand the information and integrate it into their thinking and decision-making as they serve on the board over time.

Instead, educate board members throughout a series of sessions that are fun and engaging—thus the focus on storytelling.

Good storytelling is never boring. These sessions can be organized as small group discussions before regular board meetings. If you have fewer, longer board meetings, schedule onboarding discussions before the meeting. You can also use video conferencing. Success requires discipline and a commitment not to take a short cut. This process has the additional benefit of board members getting to know one another—and that always strengthens governance.

Don't rush the sessions. Make them interesting. Use stories. Engage new members through well-developed questions.

One last tip in terms of organizing the sessions: ask seasoned board members to participate. New board members welcome the opportunity to get to know the more-experienced members, and the veteran members most often enjoy sharing what they have learned.

## Board Buddies

Before discussion of the sessions, let me touch on a mechanism that will help new members integrate and retain what they learn. Though not an orientation session, I want to introduce the concept of board buddies. The effectiveness of new board members is directly related to how comfortable and confident they feel in their governance role. They need to feel well-informed and knowledgeable. Assigning mentors—or board buddies—to new members can accelerate their learning and enable them to engage more quickly in governance and strengthen continuity.

The board buddy system works by pairing new board members with seasoned members who serve as a resource. The mentor's responsibilities include discussing board member expectations, providing background on issues and board dynamics, and answering any number of questions the new member may have about history, mission, programs, fundraising, budgeting, etc.

Some people have expressed concern to me that the mentor may bias the perspective of the new recruit, that having board buddies will create a culture of cliques, where certain board members cultivate others to take their position on issues. This fear can be addressed in many ways: ensuring transparency, encouraging independent thinking and debate, fostering open and honest conversation, cultivating a culture of integrity, and by paying close attention to who is matched with whom. I have little concern about this because it can be managed, and the value of bringing new members up to speed quickly so that they can be effective, contributing members outweighs the risk.

Once assigned, board buddies should reach out to new members right away. They should make contact soon after new members accept appointment to the board, to welcome them, thank them for joining the board, and offer to address any questions. In this first conversation, they should describe why they feel the organization is important and why they are passionate about the issues it addresses. They should also ask new members to talk about why they became involved and discuss what they hope to contribute and experience.

A second call is made before a new member's first meeting. The purpose is to inquire whether new members have questions and to encourage them to participate in the meeting discussion.

At their first board meeting, board buddies should introduce new members using their bio information, talk about what they have learned about the new member through their initial conversations, highlight what they see as new members' strengths, and describe what they see them contributing to the organization's governance. Of course, board buddies should ask new members to add anything further. This formal introduction makes new members feel welcomed and acknowledged as part of the team. It also sets expectations and implies that serving on the board is a personally rewarding experience.

Board buddies should follow up with new members after the first board meeting and their orientation sessions to discuss the new members' impressions and committee assignments. They should ask for their feedback regarding how the orientation and onboarding might be improved. New members also should be asked to offer insights about the issues facing the board. Board buddies should be sure to let new members know their participation is important and valued.

Board buddies should continue to check in with new members from time to time, particularly within a week before each meeting for the first year. The conversation will help both the buddy and the new member be more prepared to contribute to important governance discussions.

# CHAPTER 7

# Continuity—Part 2: People

## Introducing the Organization

The first onboarding session should be an introduction to the organization, which includes introducing board members to one another, providing biographies with contact information, and asking members to share stories of why the organization is important to them.

Following introductions, discuss the history of the organization, the reason it was founded, and the vision, mission, culture, and core values that guide it. As I wrote at the end of the last chapter, don't rush this conversation. Take enough time to dig in; and pose evocative questions that will stimulate deeper thinking. Then, provide perspective on the challenges that typically face the organization and the nature of its work in the community. This discussion should extend into the brand position, value proposition, strategic goals—all tied to the practical discussion of community impact.

Finally, there should be a program overview led by staff members that includes the challenges and success stories. By introducing the programs through the voices of those who deliver them, board members get a feel for the staff and vice versa.

If it is possible, bring in constituents who have been the beneficiaries of the organization's work to talk about their experiences. This should be done during the the board meeting itself, rather than just during the onboarding session. Ask them to speak with candor about how their lives have been changed. Have them talk about why the programs are important, what worked well, and even what hasn't worked well.

One of our clients works with the homeless and has hundreds of stories about changed lives. Each story is unique and moving. Storytellers express with such passion how their lives were literally saved and how the organization gave them hope and faith. Don't hesitate to mine this rich resource because it is truly the heart and soul of all that you do. You want new board members to be connected both intellectually and empathetically. It is the emotional connection that fuels passion.

## Governance Responsibilities

The second session should cover *board member governance responsibilities*. This order is quite intentional because governance makes much more sense once you know what you are governing and the challenges you might face.

Start with the meaning of the fiduciary responsibilities of governance, that is, members' legal responsibility for oversight on behalf of the public trust. These duties include the duties of care, loyalty, and obedience, and an emerging area, the duty of transparency.

The duty of care is simply that. As a board member, you take responsibility for being a well-informed participant in governance so that you can make good decisions. You attend meetings, you get involved by serving on committees and attending events, you read the materials and financial reports, and you ask good questions. By doing so, you can ensure the organization's finances are in order, that its programs are an expression of its mission, and that its constituency is served. And to do this, you must be able to employ independent judgment. That is, you make up your own mind.

The duty of loyalty means you are loyal to the obligations entrusted to you; that is, to protect the public trust. You demonstrate that you serve the organization's interest above your self-interest. You are transparent about any conflict you have in regard to that interest. Conflict of interest is common, and there is no crime in having a conflict of interest—as long as it is transparent and the interested parties act ethically and judiciously. However, self-dealing, which means taking advantage of your position of governance to obtain personal benefit from the organization, is illegal.

The duty of obedience means that you obey the law in all of your decisions and actions, and you abide by the organizational bylaws. Bylaws are the organization's statutes that govern the actions of the board. Bylaws must clearly define how the board is structured and how governance actions are taken. The bylaws should be reviewed every year so that all board members are well-informed regarding their obligations and constraints. I often encounter board members who have never read the bylaws, and I have seen boards undertake actions contrary to their governing documents. All board members should recognize that the bylaws are legal documents that they are required to follow.

In addition to bylaws, as a board member, you must ensure the organization is in compliance with all regulatory requirements, in both actions and proper reporting. Further, it means that, to the best of your ability, you make governance decisions consistent with the mission and policies of the organization.

The duty of transparency has become relevant in the last decade or so, when scandals at nonprofits like the United Way of America, Covenant House, the Foundation for New Era Philanthropy, Feed the Children, and the Hale House Foundation hit the media. Such abuses of the public trust have elicited a keen interest in transparency. This duty is the obligation placed upon nonprofits to ensure appropriate disclosure in the dealings and operation of the organization. This includes ensuring that proper information is accessible for the public, that the IRS Form 990 is accurate and filed on time, that the actions of the governing body are disclosed, and that annual reports and financials are transparent.

Beyond the fiduciary responsibilities, every board member must help the governing body function at its highest potential. Though oversight is the foundation for highly effective boards, it is only the starting place.

Highly effective boards constantly attend to strategy. They ask questions like:

- Is our theory about how our nonprofit will succeed in its mission and its ensuing practices viable? Are we having the impact we intend to have?
- Are we thinking about creative solutions and innovating in ways that will strengthen the impact we have on behalf of our constituents?
- Are we constantly challenging ourselves beyond just being relevant to being extraordinary?

- Are we asking questions that poke around the edges of "the way we've always done things?"
- Do we allow time for discussion of what might be new, different, or better?

Great board members are not just overseers; they are champions of the mission and engaged change agents. They are owners of the good, the bad, and the ugly who are committed to continuous improvement so that the organization seeks and achieves its highest potential.

Great board members, as my friend says, "drink the Kool-Aid, the whole pitcher." Having served on several boards, I observe individual board members as they approach that threshold of being "all in" for the cause. Some back away and sit on the sidelines, but those who have the spirit to step across are inspired by a passion for and a commitment to achieve the best. They hold a perspective of high expectations, and they take responsibility to make it happen. They have a mission-driven focus, a strategic approach, an unquenchable curiosity, unassailable integrity, a balanced pragmatism, and commitment to continuous learning.

These are the board members who make a difference for the mission. These are the board members who catalyze great change. These are the board members who change the future. These are the board members I want on my board.

June Broadham captured this sentiment in her book, *The Truth About What Nonprofit Boards Want*. In a cross-continent study of successful nonprofits, she found that the top characteristic of a successful board is *stellar board composition*. She went on to elaborate that board members pay attention to who is sitting at the table. On these boards, members expect to see that everyone around the table is competent and fully committed.

In terms of an onboarding session, these expectations should be made clear by the chair of the board. And this should be followed by a clear articulation of expectations and responsibilities specific to the needs of the organization.

We all benefit from reminders and clearly stated expectations. I recommend distributing to every board member a concise, clear description of responsibilities combined with an honest conversation of what is expected of every board member.

During this discussion, review the process of board member recruitment, including what competencies are sought and what you hope each new board member will bring to the boardroom. This session can close with a review of key policies (including policies that directly affect board members; such as conflict of interest, whistleblower, harassment, document retention/destruction), a review of the bylaws (particularly those that describe board member responsibilities), compliance standards (including IRS Form 990), and important dates in the coming year (particularly those where board member attendance is expected).

## Staff Roles and Responsibilities–
## Part 1: Board and CEO

The third session, *staff roles and responsibilities,* is a critical discussion and requires its own dedicated slot. It starts with a discussion of the difference between governance and management: with a sharpened focus on the difference between board and CEO responsibilities.

*I once met a board chair who hadn't grasped the difference between governance and management. She was new to the position, quite inexperienced in governance, and was also concerned about her image as a leader. Everything was going well while things were running smoothly. She was affable and engaging. Then one day, her organization's CEO encountered a significant issue with a new member of his senior management team who had a very challenging personality. As a worst-case scenario, the problem exploded into a governance-management crisis. The CEO was a veteran of the workforce and understood the situation. He immediately informed the chair of the board and worked with an external mediator to resolve the crisis.*

*When the new member of the senior management team was dissatisfied with the mediation, he contacted the board chair directly. The chair immediately contacted the CEO, directing him to handle things differently and insisted on a meeting with the staff. The CEO explained that the situation was a management issue rather than a governance issue and was being addressed through proper procedures. He reminded her of the recent mediation, provided a copy of the findings from the mediator, and shared the section of the bylaws that explicitly defined that this was a management responsibility.*

*Nevertheless, the chair and another member of the executive committee demanded a meeting with the staff, telling the CEO that he had no other option. When the CEO inquired whether this was a board decision, he was told that this was discussed among members of the executive committee. The CEO consented, under duress, to a carefully staged discussion while checking with other board members to see if the full board had been informed.*

*The chair's approach had not been approved by the board. Further, it caused great disruption to the governing board and the organization. A few of the staff members then reached out directly to the board chair, expressing their concerns. Now that she had opened the floodgate, she was unprepared to deal with it. The next board meeting erupted into unpleasantness. Some board members rightfully argued that the executive committee had not only overstepped its authority but had taken actions that disregarded, in fact contradicted, protocols outlined in the bylaws. Several board members resigned when they recognized that the bylaws had been broken and that the board's fait accompli actions had undercut the CEO's management authority causing a minor staffing furor. The chair herself resigned a few weeks later.*

There were two issues at play here. First is the issue of lack of continuity. The board chair was rather young, socially conscious, and new to the position. She had not received proper onboarding, and she had not fully grasped the responsibility of governance. When the issue came to a head, her lack of knowledge caused a short circuit. She was unfamiliar with the bylaws and the organization's established processes and procedures. She acted rashly out of an impulse to try to control the situation. But she only made things worse.

Second is the lack of proper boundaries. Because this board chair saw the board's role as managing the organization rather than partnering with the CEO, it led to dysfunction as the executive committee usurped the chief executive's role, crossing the threshold from oversight into management. It is a delicate line, but a line that must be drawn between proper oversight and management.

It is critical during this onboarding session for the CEO, with the support of the board chair, to assert her role as the executive in charge of all organizational management. As I mentioned in an earlier chapter, I tell board members that their role is to determine the "what," and the CEO's job is to determine the "how." The most effective relationship between the board and the CEO is one of governance partnering with management to ensure that the best interests of the organization are fulfilled. This does not mean that each does not challenge the other—in fact, that is necessary, but it should be done within the context of respect—with a constant focus on building and demonstrating trust.

You might say, "but the board is responsible for hiring and firing the CEO." Yes, that is true, and that is why it is important to draw clear lines.

Further, the board, not the chair of the board, is responsible for hiring and firing the CEO. The CEO does not report to the board chair. And the CEO does not report in a subsidiary fashion to the board. Rather, the CEO provides reports to the board and whatever they need to ensure proper oversight. But the board should never tell the CEO how to do her job; rather, it should tell her what needs to be achieved—and even this needs to be negotiated in good faith.

The concept that the CEO partners with the board can be traced back to its origins. The title CEO has become popular in recent years, likely migrating from the business sector. Originally, nonprofits used the term "Executive Director." This title meant that the individual was on par with the other directors, but held the executive responsibilities of managing the organization. This does not mean that the board does not hold the CEO accountable and evaluate performance. This is a critical function. However, it has to be done properly.

Back to our board story:

*After all of the unnecessary drama, the board is in a much stronger position. The new chair is an experienced board member with a calm demeanor who understands the organization, the role of governance, and the importance of policies and protocols. You might say she is plugged in and knows how all of the circuits are functioning. She immediately set about to have the board review all policies and procedures and the bylaws, so that everyone was up to speed. She is in constant contact with the CEO and shares these communiques with the board.*

*Though it took a while for the CEO to clean up the mess created by the board chair's "intervention," his years of experience have served him well. He was able to replace the member of his executive team that instigated the furor and put the organization back on course.*

## Practical Exercise

I have found the best method of ensuring proper management oversight is to create a CEO management review committee. Initiate this process at the beginning of the year. It's neither fair nor rational to make up the criteria at the time of the year-end review. The committee should comprise three board members that are acceptable to both the CEO and the board chair.

Start with the job description. Performance is based upon expectations; expectations need to be articulated in the job description. The committee should begin the process by reviewing the job description with the CEO—making amendments by mutual agreement. This does not mean redefining the job—unless it is by mutual consent and with board approval. The CEO was hired to fulfill the responsibilities as described in the position description. But as time goes by responsibilities may need to be adjusted.

Next, identify areas of responsibility. These can often be separated into the following categories: management (planning, administration, financial management, board relations, communications, fundraising, etc.); outreach (community engagement, PR, etc.); leadership (team building, vision, decision-making, problem-solving, etc.); and innovation (re-envisioning, leading change, poking around the edges of tradition to find better ways and means). What are the CEO's primary areas of responsibility? Define them. Although this is the board's ultimate responsibility, it should be done in conversation with the CEO.

The committee should ask the CEO to describe her aspirations for each area of responsibility—i.e., what it looks like if she achieves all she hopes to accomplish in this area this year. Aspiration (also known as impact) statements should be one or two sentences long—not a treatise, but a summary. Next, the committee should meet with the CEO to discuss these aspirations. The purpose of the discussion is to gain clarity of expectation, understanding, and agreement.

The third step has two parts: expectations and key activities. Ask the CEO to (i) describe what she intends to achieve in terms of measurable outcomes and (ii) identify the key activities she will undertake to achieve those outcomes. The best way to phrase a success measure is to complete the phrase, "I know I succeeded when…." This isn't a laundry list; it is a set of strategic, measurable outcomes and key activities.

A word about measurable outcomes: they include a measure and a metric that together define success. For example, the CEO writes down as a team development goal: "Grow the management competence of the senior team." This is not a measurable outcome. It's an aspiration without measurable definition. And when she reflects upon it, she might realize that growth in management competence is something that might be different for each member of the team.

Now she has a task on her hands. She lists all of the management attributes she expects down the left side of the page. They might include managing others, managing activities, managing problems, planning and organizing, getting things done, and self-management. She has a sense of what is important in each of those areas. Now she lists across the top of the page her senior team: Dewayne, Jessica, Kenneth, and Latonya. For each member of the team, where she would like to see improvement she describes what, where, and/or how.

In the real world, this process requires more than checking the boxes. I recommend individual conversations between the CEO and each of her direct reports to discuss management issues and areas of improvement so that there is a shared understanding and acceptance of the final measurable outcome.

Once this process is complete, the goal might be restated as: Each member of the senior team will develop strong competence in at least one area of management as follows:

| Team Member | Measure | Metric |
|---|---|---|
| Dewayne | Managing Activities: the ability to see what is needed to get things done on time. | Consistently meets established performance standards throughout the year as detailed in his workplan. |
| Jessica | Managing Problems: the ability to identify problems and generate effective solutions. | Demonstrates that she is proactively identifying potential problems, thoughtfully evaluating them, determining a sound course of action; as detailed in her workplan. |
| Kenneth | Planning and Organizing: the ability to set goals, build plans, and translate them into action. | Demonstrates the ability to set realistic goals, develop short- and long-range plans, and translate conceptual frameworks into concrete actions that impact program outcomes; as detailed in his workplan. |
| Latonya | Getting Things Done: the ability to focus energy on tasks and follow them to completion, dealing with stresses and strains without losing focus. | Demonstrates self-confidence, goal and results orientation, and persistence to achieve desired outcomes with consistency; as detailed in her workplan. |

It is important that during this first meeting, committee members take time to really listen to the CEO and ask good questions. That is why it is important to do this before the fiscal year cycle begins so that the conversation is aspirational, collaborative, and not defensive. But the committee should feel free to probe. Part of their responsibility is to ensure that the CEO is doing what is most important for the organization; and also to ensure that the CEO has carefully considered all of her goals, measures, and metrics. The committee should be reflective and supportive, not act as inquisitors. The primary motivation is that everyone wants the CEO to succeed.

When the process is complete, the CEO can present her plan to the board with confidence.

The committee should meet with the CEO three to four times during the year to review progress on the plan. The purpose is not to critique, but to act as a sounding board. Committee members need to be careful not to micromanage—but rather to ask good questions. This discussion should allow for changes to all aspects of the plan that are reasonable (most often, this applies to activities and success measures, much less often to areas of responsibility). Has the environment changed? Have the resources changed? Have assumptions been flawed? All of these are good reasons to adjust the plan to the current environment. On the other hand, these discussions are also intended to make corrections. If, indeed, the CEO just isn't following through on an area of responsibility, the committee should raise that issue and discuss with the CEO how it will be addressed.

The result of this process is that at the end of the year there are no surprises. All of the issues of concern have been raised during the year. This process also gives the CEO control of her destiny. She is a senior professional who defines her work plan and is accountable to the board for achieving it.

## Staffing Roles and Responsibilities– Part 2: Staff Deployment

The second part of this onboarding session is a discussion of staffing, how members of the team are deployed, and the programs they support. I recommend that staff members participate in this session so that they have the opportunity to discuss their programs with members of the board and so that members of the board get a chance to know them. Nevertheless, it is the CEO who determines whether, how, and when staff members participate.

Board members may know about the work of the organization, but when staff members walk them through their program responsibilities, they gain a deeper understanding of the nature of the work. It is most helpful when staff members use real or composite case stories, so board members get a true feel for how the organization helps people in real ways. When possible, staff members should discuss challenges as well as successes. This helps board members better understand both the opportunities and the limitations. When board members return to the boardroom, they now have a more complete grasp of the context to inform their discussions and decisions.

As I discussed earlier, the board chair should reinforce the fact that there is a clear line between governance and management and that the board must never stray into management. Further, the chair should emphasize that the CEO is fully responsible for the members of her team, and board members should not give direction or solicit requests directly to staff members without prior approval or the knowledge of the CEO.

There are instances wherein staff members liaise with board committees, but this is always at the direction of the CEO. For example, the CFO should attend finance committee meetings and prepare reports. The chief advancement officer should liaise with any fundraising committee and see that they receive guidance and appropriate administrative support. If the board conducts an audit of a program area, the CEO would likely assign a senior program officer to answer questions and provide information and data the committee needs to make informed decisions.

Finally, all organizations, at one point or another, will be faced with unhappy employees who believe they have been unfairly treated. Every organization should have a clearly stated grievance procedure. When the grievance involves the CEO, some organizations employ a professional outside mediator to look at the issues objectively. I highly recommend this approach because it keeps the board separate from management. However, in the grievance procedures, when the grievance implicates the CEO, the board is responsible for reviewing the complaint and the mediator's report and determine the proper action. This is because: (i) the CEO reports to the board, and (ii) if the grievance implies CEO malfeasance, it immediately raises the issue to fiduciary status. The chair should outline the grievance process and ensure that every board member has a copy.

# CHAPTER 8

# Continuity–Part 3: Finance and Fundraising

## Finance

The fourth board member onboarding session focuses on *finance*. This is a well-worn path of governance oversight. It usually receives the most attention because it is usually the most familiar to board members.

A primary pitfall in financial oversight is when operational efficiency and return on investment take precedence over fulfillment of the mission. Nonprofits are in a high-risk business and operate in a niche where the market cannot sustain a market-based business. Most nonprofits cannot be sustainable without government or philanthropic support. To serve a higher calling, nonprofits must rely on philanthropy, volunteers, and a team of professionals willing to relinquish high compensation.

Finance discussions should rarely be about margins and return on investment. Rather, the focus should be on a return on values.

Are the people you serve better off because you spent more money? Or is the organization better off because you spent less?

These are tough questions because the organization needs to be sustained to continue to serve its mission. I am a big fan of financial reserves, but what is the trade-off? The finance discussion should never be reduced to the bottom line of financial health alone.

This can become particularly problematic when the discussion turns to fundraising efficiency. In the last decade, self-proclaimed oversight organizations wreaked havoc on the sector, causing unnecessary harm to fundraising by focusing almost exclusively on overhead. They encouraged the public to reduce organizational effectiveness to a simple efficiency equation of the low-overhead myth.

Let's look at a hypothetical example:

*A local nonprofit prepares weekend food backpacks for kids who qualify for subsidized meals at school. These children's families may be living in poverty or living in areas of food deserts. Through the work of the fundraising team, the nonprofit receives a grant for $50,000. When all of the direct and allocated costs were added up (staff time to research, craft proposals to several foundations, phone calls, site visits, CEO time, admin support, materials), they totaled $5,000 to secure the first grant. The fundraising cost was 10 percent. Success, right?*

*However, the organization recognizes that it only served 40 percent of the families in need—let's say, two hundred families. So, the leadership team tells its fundraising team,*

*"Go get another grant!" This time it takes longer. They have already reached out through all of their contacts, including all of the foundations they knew funded in this program area. So, they purchased research software and paid for training and set-up. When they were unable to identify funding opportunities, they hired a professional grant researcher and writer, who was well versed in their work. Though part of the cost was the investment in capacity for the future—software and professional development training—it still was an outlay of cash. They succeeded in securing two grants totaling $60,000. But when all of the direct and allocated costs were tallied, they totaled $12,000.*

*Having served the most accessible families in the first round, they were now reaching out to hardest-to-serve families in more depressed communities. By connecting with community-based organizations and hiring multilingual staff members, they were able to serve many of these families. Though there were increased expenses related to staffing, professional development, and collaboration with local agencies, they were able to reach another 125 families. But the cost of fundraising has now reached 20 percent—not a good sign for the efficiency overlords!*

*One bright spot. When the mayor's office found out about what the organization had accomplished in the community, they honored them as a top community service organization for the year. They had now achieved a new level of awareness in the community, and the fundraising team was making plans to take advantage of it to find new donor prospects.*

*Even with their success, there were about a hundred known undernourished children still living in the community. So, the board and the CEO tell the fundraising team to raise more money. By this time, the team has exhausted its local foundation pool and, in consultation with the grant researcher/ writer, learns that there is a waiting period before they can re-apply. The consultant advised them to be sure to collect all of the data requested by the funders so their next proposal will be in good standing.*

*During this experience, the fundraising team has been growing in their professional acumen. What began as an events team has evolved into a foundation grants team. But they didn't stop there. After being trained by the consultant, they were now quite competent not only in foundation grant-seeking but government grants and contracts as well.*

*And they went further. A senior team member had begun attending seminars on major-gift fundraising. Through this work, and using the software they had purchased earlier, she discovered many of their board members and volunteers were rather wealthy, but no one had been asked to contribute in any formal way. Once she shared this with the CEO, he authorized her to hire a major gifts consultant to work with her team and the board.*

*Within the next few months, the team was able to secure a $10,000 government grant. At the same time, they put together a fundraising "no child goes hungry" campaign. They reached out to local merchants in the communities they were serving to promote the campaign with a poster and accept* *point-of-sale donations. The board members became actively involved and, when all was done, they had raised $50,000— at the cost of $15,000.*

*They had now much greater awareness in the community, and they were reaching the families who needed them most. It took more time and resources. But they were able to reach seventy-five more of the hardest-to-serve families. When they crunched the numbers (direct and allocated fundraising expenses), this last seventy-five were reached at a 30 percent fundraising cost!*

Was providing that nourishment to the families worth a 30 percent fundraising cost?

How would your board members look at this, financially speaking? And what would they decide to do about those additional families that are not yet served? Would they consider budgeting for the cost to build their fundraising program to expand its work? Would they view the "high cost" of fundraising as an investment— or an expense?

I have worked with housing and homeless organizations facing these types of complex problems with the same financial dilemma—how far do we go to serve those in need? One funder actually withheld funding from an organization because it claimed its grant wasn't efficiently used—even after the CEO explained the challenges in detail. The organization had to turn away people. The money was there to serve those in need—just not, in the funder's mind, efficiently enough.

This is a complex and challenging question for boards: where do we draw the line of not serving a family so that we can continue to help more people over time? And how do we conduct our own organizational soul searching to ensure we are deciding for the right reasons?

It is important for board members, particularly some of those steeped in the for-profit corporate world, to understand that the bottom line is lives… not dollars. Financials at a nonprofit organization should never be reduced to the bottom-line efficiency or return on investment. It is a much more complex conversation. This session should make that clear to board members.

## Fundraising

The fifth session is on *fundraising*. I am often questioned, "Why wait so long to introduce fundraising?" There are a couple of reasons.

Fundraising is not a governance responsibility—except for foundation boards where it is a primary responsibility because it is their mission. That may surprise some, but it is true. *Ensuring financial viability and proper use of funds* is a governance responsibility. So, here's the question: is it necessary for board members to be involved in fundraising to sustain a healthy charitable organization?

It depends on what being involved in fundraising means.

In this chapter on organizational continuity, the topic of fundraising is prone to create a short circuit. Many board members would prefer that this issue just go away. But, since it is a critical piece of organizational health and success, board members need to understand fundraising's place and their responsibilities concerning it. I learned never to point out that someone is afraid of fundraising. Similarly, I never tell anyone they shouldn't be fearful of fundraising. Instead, I will say, "the last thing I want you to do is to ask for money."

The response is often, "but we're talking about fundraising." I continue, "that is true, but the last thing you do in fundraising is ask for money." Let's discuss what is most important: all of the things you do before you ask. Most often, board members immediately think "solicitation"when the word fundraising is invoked. Solicitation is only one small part of fundraising, and most board members need not worry about asking for money.

What I want from the board is a team of passionate storytellers—which I discuss in detail in this chapter. People give to causes they believe in through organizations (and people) they trust. The heart of fundraising from the board's perspective is to learn to tell a compelling story of the cause you support through your mission. Focusing on solicitation can overload the circuit, causing it to short out. And that kills continuity.

I want board members to focus on passionate storytelling. As they do so, they strengthen continuity by learning more about the programs, the changed lives of the constituents, the successes of staff members, outcomes data, how to describe the vision, and so on. As board members continue to tell their stories, the conversation shifts from "what do you need" to "what we can do."

Suddenly a new donor is born, and the board member is not quite sure whether she even asked about a gift. People give to causes they believe in. The board member's role is to help build the band of believers, and the money will come. I will discuss this in detail in a later section.

There is research that demonstrates adding more volunteers to the fundraising equation does not translate directly into more funds being raised for the organization—but adding more trained staff does. Nevertheless, adding more volunteers does translate into *greater potential* to raise more money. This is a critical factor in growing the fundraising program. Board members are the champions of the cause and purveyors of trust who open doors and make connections that are not available to staff members.

Board members can play several important roles in the fundraising equation: investors, friend-raisers, storytellers, gift prospects, and solicitors. All of these roles relate to fundraising effectiveness. But most board members are uncomfortable with fundraising because they do not understand it. This is a problem that can be solved through a proper orientation experience and board member education.

## Investors

If you served on the board of a for-profit entity, would you buy shares of its stock? Would you invest? If not, why not? Do you not have faith in its viability? Are you there just to pad your resume? How would you be viewed serving on a for-profit board if you didn't invest in the company?

These same questions should be asked of board members who serve a nonprofit organization. Are you willing to invest in our organization? Investing financially in a nonprofit does not yield monetary return; rather, it yields an impact on the lives of those you serve. When you invest in a nonprofit organization, you are investing in promulgating values that serve a noble cause. It is an investment in the community you serve. The return is improved lives and a deep sense of doing a good thing.

A popular practice in the nonprofit sector is requiring board members to make a gift. A required gift is not a gift, it's a pay-to-play obligation in disguise. *Except* for high-profile boards populated by high-wealth individuals, pay-to-play can be harmful to the organization. It can directly conflict with the fiduciary responsibility of diversity and inclusion described in detail in Chapter 5 on board composition. It deters lower or even modest-income individuals who might add tremendous benefit by serving. Even if you make an exception to this policy, or modify it to a give-or-get policy, how would that make you feel if you didn't have the wealth or connections? Through conversations with colleagues from non-US cultures, I learned that this practice is offensive to some cultures' values, particularly how they view money and wealth.

Rather than a gift requirement policy, it is better to be transparent and talk about board members' responsibility to financially invest in the organization. As noted above, not every board member is capable of a sizable gift.

When wealthy board members are *not* giving, it is a symptom of a deeper problem. Do they not believe in the organization and its value to the community? Do they not really care about the organization and the people it serves? Do they have charitable priorities that do not include this organization? Has the staff leadership team failed to communicate the importance of board members' philanthropic support? Have the executive team and the chief development officer failed to inspire them?

People give when they have a passion for the work—when they are inspired. So, in this case, follow the lack-of-money trail. Address it directly. This means the board chair, the CEO, and the chief advancement officer need to get to know the board members. It is the responsibility of these three individuals to inspire passion for the mission and its impact that results in an investment in the cause.

When it comes to financial support from the board, the chair has a primary responsibility to set an example as a model investor and set the tone for the rest of the board. When appropriate, the chair should speak with members individually about their level of commitment. But it should be done in a manner that does not embarrass those who have limited capacity to give. If the chair of the board has limited financial capacity, an alternative is to work through a fundraising committee, preferably the committee chair. I believe every board member should participate in giving, whether it is one dollar... or several thousand dollars.

## Friend-raisers

*The other day I met with a client in the restaurant of a hotel. After the meeting, I realized that I had left my sweater on the back of the dining chair. The next day I went to retrieve the sweater, but the restaurant had closed for the afternoon. A hotel staff member was vacuuming the floors, so I said, "Excuse me, I left my sweater on a chair..." "What?" he interrupted. "I left my sweater on the back of that chair yesterday, and I was wondering..." Before I finished, he barked, "I don't know." Playfully, with a smile, I pleaded, "You don't know?" He said, "no," turned his back, and walked away. I recognize that he may have been having a bad day.*

*Thankfully, the valet captain was walking by and overheard the conversation. She said, "come this way." I said, with a wry smile, "He doesn't know." She shook her head and said, "No, he doesn't." When I retrieved my sweater from lost and found, I thought, "If I was a guest here, would I return?"*

*By contrast, recently I had a different experience at a nonprofit organization. When I arrived for a meeting, one of the security personnel came across the room. He welcomed me with a big smile and a firm handshake. When I reached the meeting room, I recounted my experience to the vice-president, who said, "We told the staff that we had big donors coming today." "It was nice that he didn't discriminate," I joked.*

*She said, "You know we are fortunate here. Everybody gets it. The other day the receptionist at the front desk came up to me and asked, 'Do you know the man that just left? When he comes here, he drives a Bentley. I think you should get to know him.'" She is the same person who remembers me when I visit and greets me with a warm, welcoming smile.*

When it comes to fundraising, everybody makes a difference. We don't know whether the person we greet might be the next big donor to our organization. But everyone throughout the organization can set the tone by being kind and responsive. The heart of fundraising is friend-raising. And we can all use more friends.

Does your board cultivate a team of friend-raisers? It isn't hard to do, and the payoff can be substantial.

## Storytellers

A friend-raiser who is a great storyteller is a killer combination. Steve Jobs believed that the most powerful person in the world is the storyteller. He excelled at it. As an old proverb states: Tell me the facts and I'll learn. Tell me the truth and I'll believe. But tell me a story and it will live in my heart forever.

We all have stories to tell from our everyday experiences, but often we don't take a moment to capture them. We learn from stories, we share our lives through stories, and the best way to raise funds is to tell stories.

I am a great fan of Matthew Dick, a high school English teacher from Connecticut. He is the winningest storyteller of "The Moth," a national storytelling competition featured on public radio. He encourages everybody to be more mindful each day in order to capture those five-second moments that are transformative. Those are the often-subtle moments when our lives are changed because of an experience.

> *One day after a concert at a local arts school that we support, we were surprised when the strings teacher introduced a young student, asking if we could take a picture with her. She said, "she has a violin because of the fund you created."*

> *That was a five-second moment. Over 80 percent of the students in that school are on the subsidized meal program. Our next gift came immediately.*

With a number of our friends, our family created a fund at Joe DiMaggio Children's Hospital to support families whose children are suffering from chronic or terminal illnesses. Here is one parent's experience of what the fund provided:

> *I participated in Art4Healing workshops at Joe DiMaggio, where my infant son lay critically ill for months in the pediatric intensive care unit. The Art4Healing workshop supported my emotional well-being as I dealt with grief, fear, and stress. It also gave me a greatly needed break from my bedside vigil and a chance to interact with other parents who have told me that they, as well as their hospitalized children, also enjoyed and benefited from the program.*

I encourage every board to engage in a storytelling workshop. It is simple to do, as I will explain below.

In addition to storytelling, make sure you have a mission moment at every board meeting. This is a five- or ten-minute segment where you share stories of how the organization has changed the lives of those you serve. If you can have constituents tell their stories, even better.

*One day when I was facilitating a board meeting, the CEO invited a woman, with two young children, to speak. She had escaped an abusive spouse and was living in a small apartment with her children. She described how she was pursuing her studies to become a nurse. When questioned, she admitted that she had to walk about a mile to the local library with children in tow to have access to a computer to continue her studies. The CEO said, "we can help underwrite her housing and modest expenses, but we are limited to that."*

*At the end of the board meeting, I had made a gift to pay for the purchase of the laptop and Internet service. Less than a thousand dollars transformed that woman's life.*

You can prime board members' imaginations by exposing them to these powerful stories. When you put together a storytelling workshop, begin by asking board members to think about what inspires them or emotionally moves them when they think about the impact the organization has on lives.

As Matthew Dicks writes in *Storyworthy: Engage, Teach, Persuade, and Change Your Life through the Power of Storytelling,* "All great stories—regardless of length or depth or tone—tell the story of a five-second moment in a person's life... and the purpose of the story is to bring that moment to the greatest clarity possible." Encourage board members to find that five-second moment... or as they get into it, two, three, or four of them. Once you tune in, it cascades into many moments.

# Practical Exercise

A storytelling workshop does not have to be complicated. The most important aspect is getting board members to tune into the emotional aspect by getting them to share how they feel about the organization. Great storytelling is not an intellectual exercise; it is an *emotional* exercise.

Start by asking each board member to take a moment to think about what they love or appreciate about the organization. After a few moments, ask them to think about, within the context of their experience with the organization, an "aha" moment, or a time when they discovered something new (about themselves, others, or the organization), or when they changed their minds, or changed their beliefs, or when they cried or laughed at something they heard, or if they were ever surprised or delighted by something they learned about the organization.

Then tell them to turn to their neighbor and tell that story— even if it's only a thirty-second story. Then ask them to think about how it changed them, whether a feeling, or a belief, or a decision, whatever. Is something different about the way they feel, think, or behave—even if it's subtle? Tell them it doesn't have to be perfect, just authentic.

In the boardroom setting, too often we get caught in our heads and forget that we are investing our time, expertise, and energy to help people and our community.

*Recently I was asked to put together a fundraising seminar for a group of doctors and administrators at a multi-billion-dollar health system. The executive was quite nervous because he was not confident that the doctors, in particular, could relate to it. I think he was concerned that they would lose confidence in the foundation team because it was so touchy-feely. I persuaded him to allow me to do it, and I promised to take all the heat if it failed. At the close of the workshop, I asked everyone to tell me what they found to be most helpful and meaningful. "The storytelling session," several agreed. The director confided, "I guess you were right."*

Another time, I facilitated this exercise with a large social service agency.

*The room was filled with board members and senior executives. I opened the session by asking the agency if a few of the program recipients could tell their stories. It worked beautifully. After they shared their stories, we transitioned directly into the storytelling exercise that I just described. As participants shared their stories, the room filled with laughter and tears of joy and appreciation. When I checked in with the CEO, he told me, "I've had that story in my head for twenty years, and I just had the chance to tell it. My board chair wouldn't let me off the hook." I discovered later that the director of advancement shared with her colleagues in other organizations how powerful the session was.*

Storytelling is easy, and storytelling that supports fundraising is powerful and fun. You just need to prime the pump and let it flow.

# Gift Prospects

While every board member should be an investor, some are also gift prospects, which means you want to cultivate significantly large gifts that are aligned with their wealth capacity. Understanding this concept (and that board members are investors) can relieve you from the odd obligation of a gift requirement or a give-and-get policy—which are often dull, blunt instruments. When you think about your board members as gift prospects, you approach them much differently—and it ups your game. It also changes how you engage them.

> *At a board meeting one evening, the staff shared news about new programs that were being introduced. There was excitement in the room and a lot of sharing of ideas. Then it came time for the development committee's report. In a bland and wonky manner, the chair of that committee dryly stated, "We have a new policy. Every board member is now required to give or get $2,500 each year." You can imagine what happened to the mood in the room.*

I keep asking myself, "Why do we do this?" Why do we view the board as a piggybank or worse, as a blood bank for a sometimes-bleeding organization? What if we respected our board members enough to treat them as gift prospects? What would we do differently?

If it were your organization, I imagine you would start by assessing the potential of board members. What is their wealth? What are their connections? What do they love about what we do? Where have they shown interest? What might be a good match for them?

Then you would craft a strategy to cultivate that interest. You would have a few conversations to explore what they believe is really important. You'd ask what they find meaningful about the organization's programs. You would ask what they'd like to see accomplished. Then, you'd pick the right project at the right time involving the right solicitor in the right setting to ask for the right amount—an amount that fits the person's means. In many cases, it would undoubtedly be more than $2,500. And it would demonstrate an authentic, thoughtful approach based upon individual interests and aspirations. I guarantee that they would contribute to the best of their abilities and enjoy doing it. And if done well, these board members would probably name a number of people they know who might have an interest as well.

I believe your board's giving will be transformed when you toss out the obligatory policy and replace it with inspired giving. Giving out of obligation has a limited shelf life. Donor fatigue is the likely result. Giving out of inspiration is giving from the heart, and it is almost boundless. It creates a ripple effect in terms of the donors' increased interest and enthusiasm.

## Solicitors

As we discussed earlier, not everyone is a solicitor. And any board member who plays this role in your organization needs to be carefully vetted. Even those who are willing to ask for money may not necessarily be good at it. So, take care in whom you ask to take on this responsibility.

Before board members can be effective solicitors, they need to feel connected and engaged. They need to intimately understand the organization and be immersed in it. In earlier chapters, I discuss how to go about this. They need first-hand experiences of the way it changes people's lives and how it improves the community. They need to have "aha" moments where they recognize that the good they want to see in the world is being accomplished through the organization they govern. If you ask board members to solicit gifts before they have experienced this epiphany, they will likely burn out, lose interest, and disengage. However, when board members are inspired by the cause and see its value and its impact, they are inspired to give and easily ask others to do the same.

My friends at Stinghouse Advertising and Marketing describe the fundraising process as "inspire, inform, invite." Great fundraising needs to follow that paradigm.

Once you have identified and cultivated the right solicitors on your board, be sure to keep them informed. Regularly discuss prospect strategies and gift opportunities. And keep them engaged in ways that sustain their interest. Make sure they have plenty of good stories to tell. Finally, be sure to talk about their success at your board meetings.

*A few decades ago, I inherited a campaign at an institution of international reach. It didn't take long for me to recognize that my campaign committee was burned out. They had been selected not for their ability to solicit or, in some cases, their connection to the campaign, but rather because of their status with the institution and their positions in the business world.*

*Campaign meetings were painful. When I arrived, we were two years into a four-year campaign that had been publicly announced, and gifts and pledges totaled less than half the goal. Many members of the committee had not made their gifts, some had refused to make gifts, and others told me they were contributing to one of the other two campaigns launched within the institution. Most, probably all, were looking for ways to run for the door.*

*I think they were relieved when I stopped actively engaging them and sought out others to lead the campaign. Engaging constituents in four major metropolitan areas, I identified the campaign leaders I needed to complete the campaign: individuals who spoke glowingly about the institution weren't concerned about formal recognition, and were ready to roll up their sleeves to make the campaign a success.*

*The momentum of the campaign shifted, and we were able to press forward. We completed the campaign on schedule and celebrated success.*

I could not have succeeded without this new group of leaders who were invested in the cause. And that is what made all the difference, not position (though a certain amount of cache is important). They were fully invested in the cause and willing to use their networks and relationships to ensure that we reached our goal.

## Fundraising and Diversity

One important point related to fundraising and diversity. When nonprofits build fundraising programs, most likely, they are not focused on diversity. They are focused on the traditional approaches because it is familiar and comfortable. No doubt, fundraising is a critical component of any nonprofit's sustainability. And with the continued growth of the nonprofit sector, there is increased competition for fundraising dollars year over year. This challenge will continue to intensify in the coming years. It cannot be ignored.

I believe there is an untapped opportunity. The demographics of our world are changing, but most nonprofits still approach fundraising from an outdated cultural perspective. What is the composition of the typical fundraising committee? My experience is that it is a lot of rich White guys and some wealthy women. For lack of a better way to phrase it, minority wealth is not accessed using the historically White donor paradigm. We need to educate nonprofit leadership to embrace a new, more diverse, culturally informed approach to fundraising.

I have read many articles on raising money from communities of color, but I have not witnessed significant change in most nonprofits' approach. We need to educate our boards and advancement officers about the beliefs and values of non-traditional donors. And they are different from culture to culture. For example, how you engage a Caribbean donor is different than a African-American donor, which is different than a Hispanic donor. Each group has its own set of beliefs about wealth and philanthropy.

Diversity and inclusion must flow over into our fundraising practices and the composition of our fundraising committees. As with those we serve, when prospective minority donors don't see themselves represented in your board or fundraising committee, they are likely less inclined to make financial contributions. A lot of fundraising dollars have not been secured simply because we have not cultivated multiple cultural perspectives and approaches. I imagine that this is a rich area for research.

## The Risk of Complacency

In closing these chapters on continuity, I'd like to shift focus to complacency, when boards get unplugged from the circuitry. This happens when a board avoids change and disruption that would contribute to its growth and ability to better serve its constituency. There are times when you have to disrupt existing practices to create a new culture.

*Years ago, I served on a very efficiently run board. Meetings started and ended on time, the founder/executive controlled the agenda, many of the board members were friends of the founder, and the chair was one of the politest people I've ever met—to the organization's detriment. Innovation was not embraced.*

*I was asked to join the board because of my professional position at the time. I suspected they thought they could use my connections to expand awareness and reach. Still, the organization served a cause that was near and dear to my heart, and I was excited to see what could be done.*

*I discovered the board was a rubber-stamp board, as the chair was complicit with the founder in scuttling anything uncomfortable. Most of the other board members didn't want to rock the boat. I was shunned when I requested an executive session without the presence of the CEO to confidentially discuss the effectiveness of the board candidly.*

*Out of frustration, three of us left within a year. One was the individual who had recruited me—a wealthy entrepreneur and former chief executive in a Fortune 500 company. Another was an individual I had recruited—a social activist and investment manager. Our leaving the board did not create the slightest ripple in the organization. Everything just stayed the same.*

In hindsight, I did the wrong thing.

The board was suffering from what I call *Xenoskepticosis* (my own word), a disease of governance in which the board is deeply ensconced in a safe comfort zone, skeptical of anything unfamiliar or unusual. It's often found in boards that have lost touch with the organization's vision or cause—the are literally unplugged. The excitement of creativity and innovation has been replaced with the ennui of habit.

*Xenoskepticosis* is highly resistant to intervention or change. The more longstanding and deeply embedded, the more impervious. Form undermines function. Comfort and convenience are valued. Risk and innovation are eschewed.

I have found that bringing about change for a board with *Xenoskepticosis* is not achieved through information or persuasion, assurances, or staff support. The cure is effected through a carefully structured recruitment process that brings change agents on board—new board members who have a passion for the cause and who understand and embrace their governance responsibilities. It requires a carefully crafted board member recruitment profile, a thoughtful and sustained recruitment process, and a sound orientation and education program that gets them plugged back in.

As this process unfolds, cultivating a consistent focus on vision and mission impact will begin to evoke consideration of new and different approaches and practices. Ideas that were previously perceived as "that's not the way we do things" are now seen as effective ways to achieve greater impact. The best way to sustain this epiphany is to structure a process of discovery rather than teach new practices. This is an opportune time to hold a board retreat managed by a skilled facilitator.

Once you have achieved this level of engagement, you have turned the corner and are on track toward a healthy recovery. Boards can get lost in the doldrums of *Xenoskepticosis* for years. But there is hope. Case in point: that board from which I resigned is now healthy and thriving.

*A new chair, someone I recruited before resigning, took the helm. This person had the perfect temperament to deal with the founder (gentle, most of the time, but firm) and was stimulated by the challenge. He had a passion for the cause, exuded confidence, and held the board accountable for governance that was mission-centered. Through his leadership, he ensured that new members were strategically recruited and focused on achieving new program and fundraising goals. He also had an uncanny ability to know which battles to fight. He once told me that his success is rooted in his ability to see the whole battlefield, not just the skirmishes.*

As you strive to achieve continuity in your board recruitment process, be sure to focus on continuous education, generative thinking, vision, and the impact of your mission, not the status quo.

# CHAPTER 9

# Collaboration

*Collaboration: working together to achieve a common goal.*

Over the many years that I have been working in the nonprofit sector, I have found that collaboration is difficult to achieve.

I'm not writing about formal inter-organizational collaboration; I am writing about the collaborative mindset. As an important side note, inter-organizational collaboration is only one of the many options organizations have to work together—and often, it's not the best option for a whole host of reasons. Someone who has written very well on this topic is David LaPiana. If you want to delve into this further, I recommend his book, *Play to Win: The Nonprofit Guide to Competitive Strategy.*

Collaboration is the mindset that enables us to work together cooperatively to advance the causes we serve.

*I was once asked to serve on the board of a newly formed theater arts organization whose mission was to use performing arts to demonstrate how to integrate the seven learning styles into student education. Given its newness, it was not well known in the community and could benefit from engaging people who could help it become more visible—and people who could open doors. I immediately began considering who might serve on the board—and other entities with whom we could collaborate to take the organization to the next level. I met with the founder to discuss what I had in mind and how these people and organizations could help. He immediately became defensive and directed me not to do anything. He was afraid and deeply threatened by the notion of bringing on people of stature or connecting with organizations who might mess with his baby.*

Fear, along with worry, doubt, and anxiety, are very common barriers to collaboration. We don't talk about them because they are perceived as weaknesses. No one easily admits that he is afraid. So, we don't look at it honestly. Yet, fear blinds us to opportunity. And many fears are evoked among board members who are not prepared, informed, or educated. The story I just told captures the fear of loss of control, a true enemy of collaboration. When you fear losing control, you cannot share.

Start by creating a safe space, an environment conducive to appreciative inquiry. As the old adage says, "good fences make good neighbors." Though this point may be disputed, in this case it is a solid solution. The first step is establishing boundaries and guidelines. Start with the bylaws. What is the extent of a board member's power, and how is it exercised? In this founder's case, I would add policies to cover the areas where he is uncomfortable. I would also outline for him the authority he retains. Use a similar process for board members who may be experiencing fear, worry, doubt, or anxiety about issues. Clarify boundaries and authority; and make assurances when and where appropriate. The goal is to protect deliberation from the influence of negative emotions.

Second, create a thoughtful engagement process. Again, in this particular case, as a board member you can introduce the founder to people in an informal setting. Help him evaluate people for integrity, passion, and general enthusiasm for his ideas—people who love what he is trying to create.

Then focus on crafting core values, building a positive board culture, and carefully managing board meetings, so are focused on the cause, not the personalities.

Knowing the cautious nature of some founders and board members, this may not be easy. But through these activities, you create the best possible environment for collaboration. Collaborative behavior can be encouraged by focusing continuously on fulfilling the organization's mission through its programs and how it can best serve its constituents. Tap into the passion the founder and board members feel for the cause. Negative emotions fade when people are immersed in their passion and see the relevance of the activity they are being asked to undertake.

Collaboration is not just about external relationships. It's also an internal mindset. How staff and board members relate to one another says a lot about whether you are able to collaborate. Does your organization have a collaborative mindset? Or is it competitive or controlling? How do staff members interact with one another? How does the CEO interact with the board? How do board members relate to one another? The culture you cultivate internally shows up externally.

At its best, collaboration is a give-and-take partnership to achieve a mutually satisfying goal. The negative emotions that I have been discussing are a primary barrier to it. (I am not suggesting that negative emotions are the only barrier; I am saying they are a very common barrier.) "What if they are stronger?" "What if they don't appreciate my vision?" "I won't let this organization be taken over by those who don't understand it." Ironically, in the story I told, no one other than the founder was even thinking in these terms. My concern was whether I could get anyone even interested in working with us.

At its core, collaboration is about trust that is rooted in shared values, competence, and capacity. Trust quickly erodes when either party fails to demonstrate that they are trustworthy… or competent. However, there are several other reasons why a partnership can fail, including style, misunderstood responsibilities, arrogance, and self-interest above organizational interest.

About twenty years ago, three researchers—Dave Logan, John King, and Halee Fischer-Wright—set out to understand how collaborative teams form. Their results, published in *Tribal Leadership: Leveraging Natural Groups to Build a Thriving Organization*, showed that collaborative, productive teams rarely form. Less than 25 percent of employee groups across all of the organizations they studied actually form effective teams. And only 2 percent form exceptionally effective teams, which they call "stage five" tribes. In fact, 49 percent of employees are individualists—many of whom might talk about the importance of collaboration but do not practice it.

The authors found that on the rather rare occasions when exceptional teams formed, they transformed their organizations. Most interesting is that those teams were motivated by what the authors describe as a *noble cause* and *innocent wonderment.*

I believe that every nonprofit is founded on a noble cause—it's called a mission. The charitable organizations we serve—especially the ones that are deeply rooted in their core values—are perfect candidates to tap into the rarified air of exceptionally effective teams. So why are so few able to achieve it?

Again, it starts with trust.

Trust is not something we possess as individuals. Rather, it is given to us by others who believe we demonstrate trustworthiness.

What do we do to demonstrate trustworthiness?

Years ago, while doing a lot of reading on the meaning of the word trust, I came across an article written by a Brit named David Masters, who wrote an equation for trustworthiness that I found fascinating. Using his equation, which accounted for a few different behaviors placed in a simple mathematical formula, one would arrive at a trustworthiness factor. What struck me about his equation is how simple it is to measure our own trustworthiness. It isn't a mystery.

Adapting his equation to something even more simple, I define trustworthiness as credibility, reliability, entrustability, and service to a greater good or noble cause. If you pay attention to these four elements every day, you will engender the trust of others—and their willingness to collaborate.

The self-appraisal questions are simple. First, am I credible? Have I done my homework? Have I conducted research and asked the right questions? Am I fully informed? And do my words and actions demonstrate that?

We have all encountered such people. They command respect from their peers, and their reputation precedes them. When they speak, people listen. They ask good questions because they are informed. And they don't hesitate to answer difficult questions because they have thought things through. For board chairs, this is particularly important. You have to do your homework and demonstrate that you know what you are talking about, that you understand the issues. Board chairs set the tone for everyone in the room.

Second, am I reliable? Do I do what I say I will do in a timely and complete manner? Do I back up my words with actions? Am I available when people need me?

There are few things more painful than counting on someone to do something important for you, and they let you down. I know it sticks with me when that happens because it's combined with self-recrimination, "I know I shouldn't have taken the risk," and frustration, "Now I have to do the job myself," or I'm left with a mess to clean up.

In nonprofit governance, we're all volunteers. We have jobs and families and other personal interests that sometimes take precedence over our volunteer obligations. Still, we have to be reliable. Once while serving on the board of a regional chapter of a national nonprofit, I agreed to chair the governance committee.

*One of our first responsibilities was to review the bylaws. We were two years out from a national reorganization of the nonprofit, and there were layers of governance issues involved in this complex, multifaceted organization. A committee was appointed and every member participated in the first teleconference. After the first few meetings, however, the task was left to two of us, a lawyer and me. Because the others were unreliable, the task took much longer as we had to research the rationale behind certain articles, talk with the CEO and the COO, check in with members of the national organization, and reference the state statutes governing nonprofits. What was most interesting to me, though, as I reflected upon it, was not my frustration that the others had bailed. It was that I expected it to happen.*

Over the years, I've seen how difficult it is to keep volunteer committee members engaged. A frequent reason is that some committees are formed out of history and habit rather than purpose. When these committees have no real work to do, people stop attending. But there are instances when the committees do very important work and need board members to be responsible and step up to the task. It takes commitment. Among many other things described in this chapter, to effectively collaborate with others, you need to be reliable.

Third, am I entrustable? Do I engender trust through my demeanor? Am I open and receptive? Do I exercise discretion? Do I keep confidences? Am I sensitive to others' concerns? Do I keep my promises?

This is one of those intangibles. It's difficult to measure, but it has such a profound impact on whether people will put their trust in you. And I've found it's not immediately evident in a person's personality. Some of the nicest people I know are gossips. I will be friendly and affable, but I won't share confidences. There are others who seem a little cranky and may be brusque, but I know that I can confide in them, that they will give me good advice, and no one else will ever know because they will keep it confidential.

Over time, entrustable people become known in an organization. And you will see people quietly confiding in them with little fuss. In the boardroom, there are often times when you might have questions but don't want to feel foolish asking them. Or you are concerned about the way something is being done, but you need to check out your thinking. Or you are just frustrated with the way things are going, so you need to let off a little steam and regain composure. Boards need entrustable people. Each of us has the capacity to be entrustable, it takes a bit of discipline to be discrete and not tell tales. And it takes a bit of practice to listen without judgment, but it is a skill that would benefit any board.

Fourth, do I value service to a greater good or noble cause above self-interest? Do I demonstrate it in my actions? Do I go the extra mile? Am I "all in" for the causes I serve?

This attribute of trust speaks to character. When I talk with boards about this attribute, I describe it as crossing the threshold to commitment. It is an intentional decision to set aside self-interest and go "all in." It means your decisions are guided by higher principles, concern for others, and complete commitment to a noble cause. Once you achieve this, some decisions come easier because you are less concerned about what it means to you—whether how it makes you look or that it means more work. These concerns fade when you have crossed that threshold. In all of my years of work with boards, those that are most effective for the cause have intentionally crossed this threshold.

Building a solid foundation of trust is fundamental to creating an environment conducive to collaboration. But it isn't "one and done," collaboration requires a daily commitment to be credible, reliable, entrustable, and focused on the greater good.

Working from this foundation of trustworthiness, there are a few other elements that are critical to establishing a true collaboration. Foremost is a deep commitment to the cause, *not the organization*, followed by clarity of expectation among all potential collaborators, clarity of boundaries (who owns what), and clarity of authority (who has what power).

## Commitment to the Cause

Sometimes when we labor hard to build something, we lose sight of the reason we built it. We have invested our heart and soul in its creation, we have made personal sacrifices to make it work, and we have worked through challenges, maybe experienced failure, as we have sought to sustain our nonprofit.

*Years ago, I served on the executive team of a health-cause agency that was founded by an individual who had contracted the disease. It's important to note that I was brand new and had come to this agency from the for-profit world, so I had no attachment to the history of the organization.*

*This individual founded his nonprofit because he knew that many lives could be saved if more people were educated about the symptoms. Research showed that early identification had a nearly 100 percent cure rate. However, the disease usually did not show symptoms until it had progressed to the point where the mortality rates were very high.*

*When I was brought on board, the organization was decades old, with tens of thousands of members in chapters across the country. Though it appeared to be thriving, funding was a constant challenge. One thing I quickly discovered was that we were competing for funding with two other organizations, one devoted to research and the other to advocacy. It occurred to me that if we could collaborate, we might be able to secure greater funding for all of us.*

*When I met with the leadership of the other two organizations, I quickly surmised that trust was an issue, but not the primary issue. As the discussions progressed, it became clear that the organizational leaders were concerned about the effect such a collaboration might have on their organizations. As I had initiated the conversation, they were further concerned that I was looking to find a competitive advantage.*

*Though we met a few more times, we progressed no further. I realized that because I had no history or attachment to the organization, my focus was on the cause and the people we served. I was open to all sorts of approaches if they proved to better serve our constituents. Since our missions were so completely different—education, advocacy, research, I saw only the advantages. But the others were entrenched in protecting their turf.*

Earlier in this chapter, I referenced the work of Logan, King, and Fischer-Wright in their book, *Tribal Leadership*. I discussed their work that showed how difficult it is to achieve collaborative teams. What their research further showed is that when most teams finally form (which is only about 22 percent of employees—the authors name this "stage four"), they have many good qualities: pride in their team, values-based relationships, and an "investor" rather than a "taker" mentality. However, they have boundaries. They create an "us" vs. "them" scenario. Even though these teams are very effective within the space they have carved out for themselves, they are limited in their capability to achieve great things because of the boundaries they have set. This is what I encountered in the story I just told.

By contrast, according to Logan, King, and Fischer-Wright, the 2 percent of teams that achieve the highest possibilities have a different mindset. As they describe in their book, people at this stage of development (stage five) express "life is great." Stage five shares the same characteristics of stage four, except that for stage five people, there is no "they." Stage five people form ever-growing networks with anyone whose values resonate with their own... The behavior of stage five expresses innocent wonderment.

The authors point out how difficult it is to sustain a stage five team. And most stage five teams over time regress to stage four, though some vacillate between four and five.

As the authors and I agree, creating a truly collaborative mindset requires a constant, palpable commitment to the causes we serve. Those causes need to resonate loudly in our hearts and minds. We must breathe it in every day if we are going to be able to rise above the obstacles we place in the way.

A passionate embrace of our noble cause is the key to engaging a collaborative mindset.

## Clarity of Expectation, Boundaries, and Authority

If we are able to establish trust, if we are able to melt the barriers that limit possibilities, it is critical that we be crystal clear about expectations, boundaries (not barriers or obstacles), and authority.

Over the arc of my career, I have worked and volunteered with people who hated clarity of expectation because it limited their options to avoid controversy and accountability. These individuals, once they achieve a certain level of power or influence, float through the years seemingly coated with Teflon. They have made an art of the subtle blame game, deftly pointing out others' shortcomings and deftly deflecting responsibility, never stepping into the trenches to dirty themselves with the difficult decisions, and untouched by failure because they avoid accountability.

Maybe it was my farm upbringing. Even as kids we were raised with a clear set of expectations, boundaries, and authority, and were held accountable for the outcomes. When we were sent out to the field to mow the alfalfa or rake it into windrows, or to the barn to stack the hay or milk the cows, or to the shed to repair machinery, we were expected to get it done. Our family's livelihood depended upon it. And it instilled me with a sense of purpose. The challenges made me stronger, and I was rewarded with a sense of accomplishment. I knew my responsibilities, and I knew what success looked like.

When I transitioned into the world of management after graduate school, I found it to be a strange place. Expectations, boundaries, and authority were mutable. I was amazed by how much energy was wasted on politics and posturing instead of productivity. As those things meant little to me, my naivety left me with a few battle scars early on, but it wasn't anything a little psychotherapy and biofeedback couldn't fix.

My second job out of graduate school taught me the power of clarity of expectation, of boundary, and of authority in creating a highly effective collaborative team.

It was actually my third job because I never started the second job. A few days after I was hired, the Director of Alumni Affairs came to my workplace and asked if I would take a different position, Associate Director of University Alumni Class Affairs. The Director and Associate Director positions were vacant, and they had no one to plan the Reunion, Homecoming, the Cornell Association of Class Officers annual meeting in New York City—and everything that went with it. Being too young to know better, I said yes.

*On a cold January day, I was shown to my office in alumni house. Though small and tucked into the back corner of the building, it had large windows on two sides. One looked over the gorge through which water cascaded over waterfalls as it flowed out of Beebe Lake, and the other looked over Trip-hammer Bridge, which students used to walk between their dorms and central campus. I felt emotionally immersed in my alma mater. But I was mesmerized for only a few moments. My assistant, a recent graduate, unceremoniously walked in, plopped down two huge three-ring binders, and said. "Here you go. We're already behind. You have five months to plan and execute the reunion."*

*At that moment, I knew it was sink or swim, and the chances of drowning were very high. It was a good thing that I lived close to campus as I spent long hours in my office. The three-ringed binders were my bible as I immersed myself in sorting out the responsibilities and tasks, the timelines, the budgets, the volunteer leaders, the campus support team, the facilities preparation, the mailings, the program of events, the keynote speakers, and what felt like a million other details.*

*It was at this point that my early learnings in life about the power of clarity of expectation, boundaries, and authority paid off. One of the greatest benefits—that I didn't realize at the time—was that I was totally, completely invested in a noble cause—the best Cornell reunion ever. I had slipped into that 2 percent stage five tribe mentality in which there is no "they." I had a campus full of people, an expansive network to connect to anyone whose values resonated with wanting the best reunion ever.*

*And I found them in hospitality, facilities, public safety, health services, maintenance, buildings and grounds, and transportation. I contacted the leaders of each department that played a part in the reunion—and it was close to every department on campus. I told them I was new to this job and I needed their expertise to make it happen. I asked if they would be willing to participate in a few planning meetings. For the first meeting we convened, the room was packed. To my deep surprise, no one had ever asked them to take part in the planning, even though the success of the reunion hinged on their performance.*

*This was years before I read Tribal Leadership and we had convened a stage five tribe that was "all in" for the noble cause. No politics, no turf protecting, no hesitation. The meetings were highly productive. Potential problems were solved before they occurred because the people who anticipated the problem and had the solution were in the room. Public safety even created a special channel on the walky talkies that we used to communicate between the central office (me) and all of our class clerks throughout campus. This had never happened before because key collaborators hadn't been asked or involved or recognized for the work they were doing to ensure a great reunion.*

*Because we had created a trusting, cause-based team, we were able to create clarity around expectation, boundaries, and authority. As we continued our planning meetings, tasks and responsibilities were clarified and assigned, as they were assigned, the boundaries between areas of responsibility were clarified, and authority for decision-making was delegated.*

*For example, hospitality and the reunion class clerks worked together closely, with the 125 class clerks reporting to five more-experienced head clerks who reported to me.*

*Hospitality was expected to deliver nutritious, delicious meals and comfortable accommodations. They hired and managed their team. They worked with the reunion class chair to determine the location of rooms and the meal menu. They had the authority to make changes and substitutions when it was reasonable to do so.*

*The class clerk's job was to manage the class activities, make sure everything was happening as it should, and solve problems for the reunion attendees.*

*Since the noble cause of all was "the greatest reunion ever," the experience of the reunion attendees was foremost in all of our minds. Because the hospitality team was on board, they were prepared to make accommodations for attendees if the head clerk requested it. This might be a different room or a different meal. If the request seemed unreasonable, hospitality would contact me, and we would reach an accommodation.*

*Because of our carefully executed planning meetings, by the time the reunion commenced, every department was clear about its expectations, its boundaries, and its authority. When I describe boundaries, I'm talking about establishing boundaries to clarify where responsibility and authority begin and end. But this did not preclude working across boundaries to help each other out. For example, one afternoon, the golf cart of one of our most generous alumni, who was disabled, stalled in the middle of nowhere. Though it was the class clerks' responsibility to take care of him, public safety and health services responded immediately to the problem. And we were able to easily coordinate this because public safety had given us our own reunion channel.*

*Apart from the $500 that alumni house was charged to install an outlet in one of the beer tents, the reunion that year was a tremendous success. Everyone collaborated from across the campus to form a team that had not been formed before. Heretofore they were just disparate parts of a thing called reunion.*

In regard to the reunion of 1982, I give full credit to all of the collaborators. They made it happen. I was just lucky enough to be on that team. I felt responsible but not "in charge." I was coaching, sometimes cajoling, and definitely intervening in a few minor crises. But, overall, it ran smoothly and was a great success.

As I wrote earlier in this chapter, collaboration is a mindset. It should be cultivated in the boardroom among all members. A collaborative mindset taps into the values that gave birth to the organization and passionately pursues mission, finds and holds fast to the innocent wonderment that invites others to join the quest, relinquishes all of the negative emotions that stand in the way, and cultivates openness, imagination, and trust.

To be sure, this doesn't mean inviting everyone. This means finding those who share your values and vision, and exemplify the traits of the high-performing team, and are motivated by the passion for a noble cause.

# CHAPTER 10

# Conclusion

Conclusion: the last part; or an opinion reached after considerable thought.

Highly effective boards are governed by people who are champions of their nonprofit's cause, servants of the public trust, and skilled in nonprofit governance. These champions ensure that the nonprofits they serve stay true to their mission and thrive. They are individuals who have crossed the threshold to be "all in" and are fully invested in a noble cause. They understand what it takes to build and sustain a highly effective board and are invested in its success. They devote significant time and energy to recruitment and onboarding.

There are a number of boards focused on governance, yet they lack discipline in their recruitment practices. When we discuss recruitment with some of these board members, they tell us they can't find qualified candidates. When I ask them to describe the qualifications, they tend to be vague and uncertain.

My advice? If you know what you are looking for, it's much easier to find it.

The purpose of this book is to dig deep into the characteristics that define champions, those who embody what it takes to excel at governance. It is also intended to provide practices that boards can adopt that will sustain continuity of effective recruitment and onboarding practices.

Board member recruitment and onboarding—including education—should be an ongoing, core governance practice. Every board should form a committee responsible for identifying and articulating prospective member characteristics, developing the profile, facilitating board discussions to identify candidates, vetting the candidates, interviewing the candidates, orienting the candidates, overseeing the board buddy mentors, and ensuring that new members are fully educated as they join the board.

During the recruitment process, treat each candidate as though she is about to fill the highest office in the organization. Because it's true.

Thoughtfully managing board recruitment and onboarding is the most powerful tool you have to create an effective board. Paying attention to the seven principles will ensure that you address the most important elements.

In closing, I would like to provide a board self-assessment exercise. For each of the principles I have discussed in this book, I provide a self-rating scale. I suggest each board member and the CEO complete this assessment individually and then discuss perspectives as a group. It is important to agree upon the definition of both the problem and successful resolution before you can make progress.

It seems obvious to begin making improvements by starting with the items that receive the lowest rating. However, the board might find that even though an item is rated higher, it is causing serious consequences that must be addressed first. My advice is to start where you can make an impact right away. The experience of success is a great motivator.

Turn the page to start your board assessment.

# #1 Culture

Every organization and every board have a culture: the unspoken assumptions about how people should think, feel, and act—and the behaviors that result from those assumptions.

Developing a productive culture is critical to building an effective board. Culture arises out of core values, the soil in which the organization is rooted. Core values determine how we think, feel, and act. They are the substrate out of which all decisions arise. Culture can be managed through understanding, articulating, and constantly aligning with core values that the leadership determines best capture the heart and soul of the organization.

Healthy cultures are inquisitive; they invite diverse perspectives and debate. They embrace generative and strategic thinking. Innovation is valued. In healthy cultures, board members work collaboratively and with humility to solve problems. Members understand their governance oversight responsibilities. They respect the role of management and form a constructive partnership with the CEO. They are intellectually and emotionally invested in the cause they serve and are its champions.

| 1 | 2 | 3 | 4 | 5 |
|---|---|---|---|---|
| We have not considered the impact of culture on governance. | Our culture is dysfunctional and counterproductive. | Our culture limits board productivity; we are lacking in a number of areas. | We strive for good governance, but our culture is not there yet. | Our culture is intentional and rooted in our core values. |

What needs to change?

- 
- 
- 

What does success look like?

What are the next steps?

1.

2.

3.

# #2 Character

In the boardroom, character counts. How board members conduct themselves influences the effectiveness of the board as well as the community's perception of the organization.

By interviewing prospective board members for character—validating it through research and interviewing references—and reinforcing expectations explicitly, you not only strengthen the cohesiveness of the board as a governance team, but also insure the organization against disreputable behavior and bad press.

How board members conduct themselves in business, civic, and social life reflects on the organizations they govern. How board members treat one another in the boardroom is crucial to creating the right atmosphere for productive discussion and decision-making. Members need to respect and trust one another, show integrity, and act maturely and responsibly. They should exude a commitment to and passion for the organization's cause, value service above self, and work collaboratively to fulfill the fiduciary duties entrusted to them.

| 1 | 2 | 3 | 4 | 5 |
|---|---|---|---|---|
| We do not consider character in our recruitment practices. | We want members to behave well, but we do not pay much attention to it in recruitment. | We agree that character counts, but don't have an intentional recruitment practice. | We interview candidates and judge character based upon impressions and their rep in the community. | We define what character means for our board and carefully vet candidates. |

What needs to change?

- 

- 

- 

What does success look like?

What are the next steps?

1.

2.

3.

# #3 Competence

In board recruitment, we often confuse credentials with competence. We look for business acumen or accomplishments when we should look beyond them to the person's ability to govern effectively.

When board members are competent at governance, they grasp the issues and the context, think clearly and carefully, and make well-founded decisions that serve the best interests of the organization and its cause. Competence is the ability to think—IQ, EQ, or CQ, communicate, and demonstrate sound judgment. Other important competencies include governance knowledge and aptitude, a sense of humor, patience, knowledge of how things work, and a grasp of the subject matter that forms the basis of the organization's programs and activities. Some board members develop their competencies as they serve, learning as they go. Most importantly, the board must demonstrate that it values competence among board members and supports its development.

| 1 | 2 | 3 | 4 | 5 |
|---|---|---|---|---|
| We do not consider board member competence in our recruitment practices. | We give little attention to competence in our recruitment practices. | We look at experience and community service; but do not evaluate competence explicitly. | We give thought to what we need and judge board member "fit" during the interview process. | We define the competencies we seek and carefully vet candidates. |

What needs to change?

- 

- 

- 

What does success look like?

What are the next steps?

1.

2.

3.

# #4 Connections

Connections are important to effective governance. But an organization doesn't just need connections, it needs members who are willing *and* able to use their connections for the good of the organization and its constituents. Most often, boards are looking for members who have access to wealth. This is important, but a board also needs connections to the people it serves so it truly understands their needs; to those who are influential, so it can position itself within the community and develop prominence; and to those who are uniquely positioned to help it succeed, so that it can continuously improve its programs and services.

| 1 | 2 | 3 | 4 | 5 |
|---|---|---|---|---|
| We do not consider board member connections in our recruitment practices. | We give little concern to connections in our recruiting process. | We have some idea of the connections we need, but it is given little forethought. | We consider connections when we recruit candidates, and touch on it in the interview process. | We annually assess our needs for all types of connections and carefully vet candidates. |

What needs to change?

- 
- 
- 

What does success look like?

What are the next steps?

1.

2.

3.

# #5 Composition

Building a competent, diverse, and inclusive board takes commitment and hard work. Though diversity is essential in board member recruitment, it should not supersede competence. Diversity and competence must go hand in hand. Diversity without competence is tokenism. Competence without diversity fails to fulfill the fiduciary responsibility to serve the public trust. It fails to serve our communities, our society, and each other.

Charitable organizations can provide leadership by creating recruitment practices that embrace diversity and inclusion. Recruit board members for the contributions they can make to governance and, through attention to diversity, you enrich board member engagement and board culture.

Seek out only those who are best qualified to serve, use the filter of diversity to make your choices, and practice inclusiveness intentionally.

| 1 | 2 | 3 | 4 | 5 |
|---|---|---|---|---|
| We do not consider competence, diversity and inclusion in our recruitment practices. | We talk about competence and diversity, but do not follow through in our recruitment practices. | We consider competence and diversity in our recruitment practices, but results have been hit or miss. | We have clear intentions to create a competent and diverse board—but no policies—and have had some success. | Our policies and practices support building and sustaining a competent, diverse, and inclusive board. |

What needs to change?

- 
- 
- 

What does success look like?

What are the next steps?

1.

2.

3.

# #6 Continuity

When there is continuity, the organization hums with efficiency and effectiveness. Continuity results from a rigorous onboarding process that provides board members with an understanding not only of their governance responsibilities but also of how everything in the organization works and is interconnected. In short, it's organizational knowledge and intelligence.

Knowledge and intelligence are fundamental to sustaining continuity within a governing board. It requires an ongoing, intentional process of education, engagement, and trust-building. It requires vigilance and the discipline of ongoing board member education.

| 1 | 2 | 3 | 4 | 5 |
|---|---|---|---|---|
| We do not have an onboarding and board education process. | We distribute an information packet to new board members. | We distribute a packet of materials to candidates and provide new members with a board manual. | We distribute a board member manual, host an orientation session or two for new board members, and host a few board education sessions. | We have a carefully constructed board member onboarding and education program; and assign board buddies. |

What needs to change?

- 
- 
- 

What does success look like?

What are the next steps?

1.

2.

3.

# #7 Collaboration

When I use the word collaboration, I mean the mindset that enables us to work together cooperatively to advance the causes we serve.

At its best, collaboration is a give-and-take partnership to achieve a mutually satisfying goal. At its core, collaboration is about trust that is rooted in shared values, competence, and capacity.

Creating a truly collaborative mindset requires a constant, palpable commitment to the causes we serve. It needs to resonate loudly in our hearts and minds. We must breathe it in every day if we are going to be able to rise above the limitations we set for ourselves.

A passionate embrace of our noble cause is the key to engaging a collaborative mindset.

| 1 | 2 | 3 | 4 | 5 |
|---|---|---|---|---|
| We do not consider collaboration in our board practices. | We do not seek out collaborative opportunities. | We explore opportunities to collaborate when they present themselves. | We value collaboration, especially within our organization. | We focus on our noble cause and invite those who share our vision to work cooperatively to achieve a greater good. |

What needs to change?

- 

- 

- 

What does success look like?

What are the next steps?

1.

2.

3.

# Epilogue

It has now been forty years since that summer afternoon when I was first asked to speak with members of a nonprofit governing board. I have been unusually fortunate to have found a cause-based career, wherein the work has been meaningful and interesting year after year.

In writing this book, one of my concerns is that people might think I'm taking all the fun out of volunteering to serve on a board because it takes so much work and commitment.

My response is yes, it does. Governance is serious business that requires a significant investment of energy and time. It requires you to cross a threshold of commitment and be "all in" for a cause. But, once you do, once you give it your all, you open up to an opportunity to have a deep and meaningful experience. Yes, board service comes with plenty of challenges and frustrations, but giving yourself to a cause larger than yourself is fulfilling in a way that is hard to describe.

Maybe the true meaning of serving on a board is making an offering. An offering of yourself to achieve a greater good. As Peter Senge wrote, "That choice (to serve) is not an action in the normal sense—it's not something you do but is an expression of your being." To me, there is no greater sense of satisfaction than investing ourselves wholly in a great cause.

# Index

# V

. CPSIA information can be obtained
at www.ICGtesting.com
Printed in the USA
BVHW041639030121
596793BV00018B/158/J

9 781734 297317